Easy to Make Inlay Wood Projects— INTARSIA

by Judy Gale Roberts and Jerry Booher

A Complete Manual with Patterns

FOX CHAPEL PUBLISHING
Box 7948J · Lancaster, PA 17604

Look in the back of this book for a complete listing of available patterns by Roberts Studio.

©1993 , Fox Chapel Publishing

Manufactured in the United States of America

ISBN #1-56523-023-X

Color Photography:Bob Pollett / VMI Productions, Leola, PA

*Cover and Interior Design / Typesetting:
Mouse Pad Studios, Lancaster PA*

*To order a copy of this book
please send cover price plus $2.50 :*

**FOX CHAPEL PUBLISHING
Box 7948 J
Lancaster PA 17604**

Please try your favorite book supplier first!

"Safety First"

Before getting started we want to urge you to develop good safety practices any time you are using any type of woodworking machinery or hand tools, as well as using good common sense when using finishes of any kind. Please make safety glasses and hearing protection standard procedure when using any type of machinery.

Be sure to read and follow manufacturers recommendations for power tool safety, as well as to read and follow the safety recommendations for the use of finishes (good ventilation and lots of it!)

Table of Contents

About Judy Gale Roberts

My parents, both aspiring to be great artists, met while attending art school in New York. They married and moved to Texas, where my father, Pat Dudley Roberts, was a freelance artist. He worked with architects and designers creating artwork for commercial projects, and occasionally he also accepted private commissions. When I was growing up, there was always some creation in progress in the garage or in my father's studio. My mother, Marilyn, was very inspirational, always offering helpful advice.

Growing up in this environment left me little choice about what I wanted to be when I grew up. In fact, it wasn't until high school that I realized that my art skills were different from those of other kids my age. I just thought most kids didn't try very hard or care what their work looked like; I finally realized that they were doing their best.

I have always enjoyed sculptural art forms more than painting. I like feeling things—different textures—and being able to form things with my hands. Until I started intarsia, I worked mostly with clay.

When I came of age, I chose an apprenticeship with my father over art school or college; I felt it would be the most valuable to me. (Everyone in the family worked with my father at one time or another.) At that time. we worked in many different media. Wood was a material we used only occasionally, in conjunction with something else.

In the late 1970s, we made our first project entirely of wood. These large wildflowers were intended for the atrium of a bank, where they were to hang 20' off the ground. The flowers, some of which were 4' or 5' in diameter, were rough cut and did not have much color variation, but they did have dimension. Since everyone who saw these flowers admired them, the next job followed.

That job involved designing and producing woodland scenes of animals and trees—for a restaurant called "The Woods." We were to make two 4'x 8' panels; one 6' x 6' double-sided panel (the same scene on both sides) with cutouts one could look through, like a screen; and a smaller panel with the restaurant's name inlaid, to hang by the entryway.

My father did all the design work for this job and I helped enlarge his designs, transfer them to the wood, cut parts, sand, and glue the work down. At that time we were playing it by ear in terms of procedures. We didn't make a complete pattern for each panel, showing the entire design. Instead, we pieced the scenes together. We made individual patterns for the animals and some of the other elements. Then we filled in the empty spaces with mosaic-like pieces of wood. These give wonderful texture to a scene and provide the artist great freedom of shape. But you can imagine how much time it took to cut out all those mosaic pieces, not to mention to glue them down. That's one reason we began making more complete patterns—and substituting solid pieces of wood for the mosaic work.

The projects were roughly sanded, with a low relief. We glued them down before we applied the finish—several thin coats of spray lacquer.

When my father and I were doing this work, we called the technique wood murals. We did not find out until years later that what we were doing had an "official" name—intarsia.

My father and I used mainly Western red cedar. The more I worked with the cedar, the more I began to notice the variety of shades this wood has—and even the variations of shade within boards. Since I was doing most of the layout at that time (my father did most of the sawing), I started to experiment with wood color and grain direction. From then on, when we went on a buying trip to the lumberyard, we were looking for more than just Western red cedar. We wanted a palette of colors.

In the mid-1980s, Jerry Booher and I began to work together. We scaled down the size of the finished pieces and began exhibiting at arts and crafts shows. I showed Jerry how my father and I had made the wood murals. After working on a few projects using those techniques, Jerry started recommending different approaches. At first I was reluctant to believe that Jerry could come up with anything better than what my Dad and I had developed. I finally had to admit, though, that Jerry had some very good ideas—and I started to see things his way. Combining his skills and experience with mine, I feel we have worked through most problems that arise when doing intarsia.

At the shows, Jerry and I were asked countless times, "What do you call this?" These questions inspired Jerry to write to the National Wood-Carvers Association, sending them pictures of what we do and asking that same question. To my surprise, the association had a name for it—intarsia. At first I did not want to believe it; I preferred thinking this form was something my father had "invented." But in time I grew to like the idea that our work had a legitimate name.

Once I found out its name, I decided to do some research on intarsia. I wanted to see for myself if what we were doing was really intarsia. With my curiosity aroused, I was a bit disappointed. Very little has been written about intarsia, and few pictures of the really early works are available. From what is available, however, I can tell that what we are doing is similar to what the early craftsmen produced. One difference is that our work is dimensional; theirs is not. That is understandable given the limitations of their tools. Cutting through 2" thick material with any accuracy with a knife is next to impossible.

As a craftsperson, it's a nice feeling to know that you have a link with the past—that you share with craftsmen of the fifteenth century some of the same wonder of wood.

About Jerry Booher

I was born and raised in Springfield, Ohio. At an early age, my father, John Booher, began to train me in mechanical things, and I became a general machinist and tool maker. Before hanging up my micrometers in the mid-1980s, when I began to work with Judy, I spent 20 years working in job shops in Ohio, Pennsylvania, and Texas.

I'm largely responsible for the "fit and finish" of our intarsia projects. Judy is the creative talent.

Sometimes I still can't believe my eyes when I see one of our projects completed. It seems like they just happen. I know Judy has a picture in her head of the end result as we work on a project, but I have to take a "wait and see" attitude. I'm mechanical, without an artistic bone in my body.

Working with Judy has been a wonderful experience. I feel very lucky to be so closely associated with such a great talent. Watching the popularity of intarsia grow, partly because of our efforts, is also very rewarding.

Intarsia: A Brief History

From the earliest times, wood decoration methods fall into five categories: painting, gilding, engraving, carving, and intarsia. The ancient art of intarsia—the making of decorative and pictorial mosaics by laying precious and exotic materials into or onto a groundwork of solid wood—inspired both marquetry and inlay.

Through the centuries, rich patrons employed craftsmen to create beautiful works of art from wood. Works of this sort are seen in the histories of ancient Egypt, imperial Rome, Persia, eighth-century Japan, and fifteenth and sixteenth century Germany and Italy, where the best examples are found. The traditional process, involving many long and demanding steps, was both expensive and painstaking. First, rare and exotic hardwoods had to be imported at great cost. Then the groundwork was slowly carved, lowered, and trenched. Next the precious but difficult-to-cut hardwood was sawed and sliced into 1/4" to 1/2" thick tiles and these mosaic tiles were fit and set, one at a time, in a bed of glue or mastic. Finally, the inlaid surface was scraped, rubbed down, waxed, and burnished.

According to Italian authorities, the word intarsia is derived from the Latin verb interserere, "to insert." These authorities classify intarsia works as "sectile" (in which fragments of wood or other materials are inserted in a wood surface) and "pictorial" (in which pieces of wood completely cover a ground). As in modern intarsia work, the wood slices were attached with glue.

Historians agree that the city of Siena was the cradle of Italian wood carving and inlaying. As early as the thirteenth century, documents mention a certain Manuello who, with his son Parti, in 1259 worked on the ancient choir of the Siena Cathedral.

Domenico di Nicolo, one of the finest Sienese masters of intarsia and carving, worked for 13 years on the chapel in the Palazzo Pubblico at Siena, using some of Taddeo Bartoli's designs. di Nicolo's work also included the doors of the Sala di Balia

Intarsia work was also made at an early date at Orvieto, but the craftsmen were all Sienese.

In Italy, where the techniques are more than a hundred years older than in other European countries. Intarsia was originally made by sinking forms into wood, following a prearranged design, and then filling in the hollows with pieces of different colored woods. Initially only a small number of colors were used. Early writings indicate that the only tints employed were black and white, but this must be interpreted broadly. The color of wood on the same plank usually differs from place to place; tinting would not have obscured the variations in wood color.

In the early fifteenth century, at the beginning of the Italian Renaissance, the intarsiatori produced graceful arabesque works perfectly suited to the raw material and often executed with perfection. These works are considered by some to be the most entirely satisfactory of their works, although not necessarily the most marvelous.

After the invention of perspective drawing and its application to painting, ambitious intarsia crafters emulated this representational trend in wood. Much of their work focused on street scenes and architectural subjects (not always very successfully) and simple objects like cupboards with their doors partly open to show items on the shelves (often extraordinarily realistic considering the materials and techniques used). This focus on realism was assisted by Fra Giovanni da Verona's discovery of acid solutions and stains for treating wood (to produce a greater variety of colors) and by the practice of scorching areas of the wood to shade them, suggesting roundness.

In the best works of the period, pear, walnut, and maple were the principal woods, although pine and cypress can also be found. A tincture of gall apples was used to imitate the color of ebony.

Although fame might be won by the exercise of this demanding—but slow and tedious—craft, the winning of fortune was a very different thing. Even in Siena, a flourishing town that prided itself on its reputation for fine wood craft, it was difficult for the craftsmen on whose work that reputation depended to make a living. At one time, Florence had 34 workshops for wood carving and intarsia. It can be concluded that work of a certain sort was plentiful and lucrative—and intarsia panels were sometimes exported. However, the most celebrated intarsiatori also practiced some other form of art and sooner or later abandoned intarsia altogether.

Early intarsia works depend mainly on silhouette for their beauty, but they also exhibit the use of line (made by graver or saw) within the main composition. A great deal can be accomplished by choice of wood type, color, and tone and by arrangement of grain direction. Some of Fra Giovanni's perspectives show very suggestive skies made in this manner, as well as representations of veined and colored marble and of rocks. When the human figure entered into the design, however, inner lines were essential. Wood color and grain were not sufficiently expressive.

The craftsman's aim is to display the qualities of the material with which he is working to best advantage, consistent with the purpose of his work. Pride in overcoming the limitations of the material to achieve an aesthetic vision can at times sway the artist from this course. In any craft the marriage between the material and the vision—the presence of an intelligent designer—should be paramount.

On the subject of intarsia design, Stephen Webb has said:

"Tone harmony, and in a limited degree, the sense of values, [the artist] must certainly cultivate. He must be able to draw a line or combination of lines which may be ingenious if you like, but must be delicate and graceful, vigorous, and in proper relation to any masses which he may introduce into his design. He must thoroughly understand the value of contrast in line and surface form, but these matters, though a stumbling block to the amateur, are the opportunities for the competent designer and craftsman. The most charming possibilities of broken color lie ready to his hand, to be merely selected by him and introduced into his design. If the wood be properly selected, shading is rarely necessary, and if it is done at all should be done by an artist. In the hands of an artist very beautiful effects may be obtained, the same kind of wood being made to yield quite a number of varying shades of color of a low but rich tone. Over-staining and the abuse of shading are destructive".

Sources: Jackson, F. Hamilton. Intarsia and Marquetry. London: Sands & Co., 1903.

Hawkins, David. Techniques of Woodworking. Sterling.

Chapter 1

Wood Selection

Wood Selection

In creating an intarsia project, the two most important aspects of wood selection are wood color and wood grain configuration. Comparing intarsia with painting, you could liken wood color to choice of paint colors, wood tone to mixing of paint colors, and wood grain to types of brush strokes. Looking at an intarsia work (or a painting) from a distance, the colors stand out the most. Under closer inspection one begins to see how the grains (brushstrokes) work in each area. Add dimension—a characteristic intarsia has that painting really does not—and you begin to realize that intarsia employs at least three skills, those of a cabinetmaker, a painter, and a sculptor.

Lumber Thickness and Board Width

I purchase lumber in standard thicknesses: 1"and 2". Of course, a nominal 1" board is actually anywhere from 5/8" to 3/4" thick. A 2" board is between 1½" and 1¾" thick. If you are just beginning with intarsia, I recommend starting with 1" thick lumber. It is both easier to cut and to find than the 2" thickness.

I look for the widest boards available. Generally, I buy 1" x 12" or 2" x 12" boards. (There always seems to be at least one part in an intarsia pattern that will not fit on lumber 6" or less wide.)

It takes a while to build up a wood inventory for intarsia. One trip to the lumberyard may yield only light wood; the next may turn up all medium shades. If you can afford to do so, keep your inventory up. When you've decided to start a new project, it's frustrating to discover that you've run out of a shade you need, must make a trip to one or more lumberyards to find the right board, and then must wait for your new board to dry before you can use it.

Wood Species

For intarsia, I generally use Western red cedar (WRC). It is easy to find this species locally and the wood itself varies in shade, from an almost white color (the sapwood) to a deep brown. Of all the shades, the WRC sapwood can be difficult to find, and when I do locate some, it is generally only 2" or 3" wide (Illus. 1-1). I often substitute white pine, basswood, or jelutong (a wood from Indonesia) for the white WRC sapwood.

Other intarsia buffs use a variety of wood species. They are grouped by general color below, but the color can vary some:

White:	poplar, basswood
Light to medium light:	ash, aspen, birch, hickory, maple, sycamore
Medium to medium dark:	beech, aromatic red cedar, cherry, mahogany, pecan, redwood
Dark:	walnut

Western Red Cedar
The majestic Western red cedar (WRC) is native to western North America. It's found along the coast from southeastern Alaska to northwestern California and also inland in a section of the Rocky Mountains from southeast British Columbia to northern Idaho.

In the wild WRC prefers rich soils with abundant moisture. In that climate, mature trees are massive, with flared bases and weathered reddish brown bark that is stringy and fibrous. Trees can reach heights of 190 feet (60 meters) with diameters exceeding 6 feet (2 meters).

A slow-growing, naturally durable tree, the best WRC specimens are found in the British Columbia coastal forest. In fact, WRC accounts for more than 20 percent of the mature forest resource there and has the longest life span of any tree in that forest. WRC is considered one of Canada's most beautiful and durable species.

Freshly cut WRC is strongly aromatic and reddish brown in color. With exposure, the wood turns a dull brown.

The fine grain, decay resistance, and rich coloring that are trademarks of WRC are the result of its slow growth and natural oily extractives. The narrow sapwood is a light straw color; the heartwood, a blend of warm earth tones ranging from a pale yellow through a reddish pink to a chocolate brown.

Lightweight and soft-textured, WRC is a stable wood that seasons easily and quickly, with little shrinkage. Its insulation value is higher than that of most other woods due to its low density and particular cellular structure.

WRC is easy to work with either hand or power tools. It planes to a smooth, rich, lustrous finish. It cuts or splits easily along the grain; hence, its widespread use for roof shingles and shakes.

Because it is free from pitch and resins, WRC has excellent finishing properties. It accepts both semitransparent finishes that reveal the wood's warm colors and textures and full-bodied paints or stains well. It also has good gluing qualities and nailing properties.

Much myth and legend surrounds the WRC. West Coast Indians used it to make clothing, baskets, lodges, canoes, and totem poles. Western red cedar is also called the giant arborvitae, or "tree of life."

WRC is weather and insect resistant. For this reason, it is commonly used for fencing, siding, decks, and other outdoor uses. When dry, it is lightweight and easy to handle. Most lumberyards stock it for a variety of end uses.

Board Selection

When dealing with a lumberyard for the first time, I bring along pictures of what I do, ask if I may pick out my own lumber, and explain that I want the boards with knots—that I am not picking out what the yard considers "premium" lumber. I also leave the lumber stacks in better shape than I find them. Most lumberyards do not mind us picking out the wood ourselves—and then letting them know what we found. Occasionally, after the staff at a yard knows what I do, someone will come out and start picking out different colors to show me. When I'm shopping for wood, I look at every piece of WRC the yard has; few boards go unturned. I often find the largest variety of colors in the fence picket pile.

Here's the procedure Jerry and I use. With one of us at each end of a stack of lumber, we move one board at a time and check each one. (Usually, the best board for our needs is the one on the bottom!) As we go through the stacks, I look at the boards for color and for grain pattern. A board that varies in color from a light to a medium or from a medium to a dark shade is useful in creating depth or shading in areas of an intarsia composition. For example, if a project has some hills in it, you can cut those hills from a board that varies in color, using the light area for the hilltops (Illus. 1-2). This technique adds depth to the hills, making them appear rounded from a distance even though they are flat. So, when I see boards with light or dark streaks or a gradual shading from one tone to another, I buy all I can.

Sometimes, especially with 2" thick lumber, one side of a board will be light colored and the other side will be dark as walnut. You can take advantage of this natural occurrence by planning ahead when you lay out your intarsia project. When you sand or carve into a board like this (Illus. 1-3), you know the recessed areas will be a darker color, creating a shadowlike appearance in your project. You might use a board of this sort for hair; when you expose the dark wood by carving or sanding, the recessed areas will be darker, giving depth to the hair. This technique eliminates the need to cut a dark piece of wood for that area of the composition. Learning to use the natural characteristics of wood in this way not only produces a more interesting finished project, it can save you time.

Sometimes a piece of lumber will itself inspire a project. You might look at a streaked piece of lumber and see a sunset. I purchased a board with a grain pattern that resembled alligator hide. I set it aside until I had time to create a new intarsia design with (you guessed it!) an alligator as the subject matter. When the time came, I cut the alligator's body from that board.

After you work with intarsia a while, you will never look at a board in the same way. Even if you previously appreciated the beauty of wood,

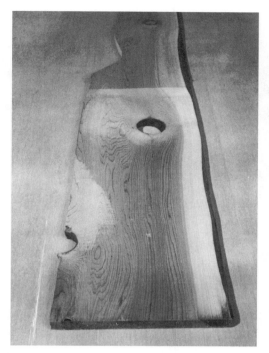

Illus. 1-1. The sapwood of Western red cedar, seen along the right section of this board, is almost white. It can be difficult to find, and segments are generally narrow, as in this example.

Illus. 1-2. Note the color gradations in the wood used to cut the hills in the foreground of this intarsia scene. The wood at the bottom of each hill is darker than the wood at the top, giving the effect of light and shadow and making the hills appear rounded, even though they are flat pieces of wood.

you'll begin taking a new look at every bit of wood in your house (furniture, paneling, doors).

Wet or Kiln-Dried?

We have purchased WRC two ways: wet and kiln-dried. Provided we have ample time to dry it, we prefer to purchase our wood "wet." The reason is simple: WRC has a tendency to dull in color slightly when it is dry. This makes it difficult to select just the right color for your needs, especially when you are looking for a medium light shade to go with a light piece or trying to distinguish a medium dark shade from a dark color.

Illus. 1-3. Some boards, especially thicker ones, may be lighter on one side than they are on the other. Sanding or carving into the board exposes the darker shade. Take advantage of this natural characteristic of the wood to create highlights and shadows.

Illus. 1-4. Applying even a clear finish to wood (as has been done on the left side of this piece) darkens the wood one or two shades.

In the wet state, WRC shows its true color more accurately. It is close to the color it will be when you have sanded it and applied the finish. When the wood is wet, the grain also has more contrast, making it easier to see grain patterns.

If you are new to intarsia and anxious to get started on a project, kiln-dried WRC can be a good choice. However, the kiln-dried boards in most lumberyards are predominately straight grained, lacking the unusual grain patterns we prefer. Kiln-dried cedar is also quite a bit more expensive than wet wood and can be harder to find as well.

Wood Color

It's important to have at least four shades of wood available in your inventory. I prefer to keep five or six shades handy: white, light, medium light, medium, medium dark, and dark.

As you consider a board for purchase, remember that the color of wet WRC is very similar to the shade it will be after it is sanded and sealed. Applying a clear finish to the wood always darkens it a shade or two (Illus. 1-4).

WRC that has been in the lumberyard for a long time is generally gray and discolored. In this condition, it is difficult to tell what tone the wood is. With boards like these, I first look at the grain pattern to see if the board warrants more attention. If the grain pattern is unusual, I might carve a small sliver from an edge to get a better idea of the wood's color. Often, if the grain pattern attracts me, I will take a chance and buy the board. Many of these boards are like buried treasure; if they turn out not to be exactly what you want, they still make good shelving!

If you cannot find wood in all six shades or if you are just beginning with intarsia and do not want to "practice" on the more expensive woods, create your own palette of colors. Purchase white wood and stain it to various degrees of darkness. With this method, you can still use grain direction and grain patterns to advantage.

Grain Patterns and Direction

In intarsia, grain patterns work on the viewer at a somewhat unconscious level, helping to move the viewer's eye to follow the composition of the piece. Because some woods pick up light differently when turned at different angles, you can create the illusion that the wood pieces are different colors (Illus. 1-5). You can use this property to create subtle effects in selected areas of your composition.

Some intarsia buffs believe that all the grains in a composition should move in the same direction—that contrasts in grain direction are distracting. I disagree with that notion. My feeling is, why limit yourself? Many intarsia projects that look dimensional from a distance are, on closer inspection, actually flat. Grain direction alone gives certain parts of the composition the appearance of depth.

For your wood inventory, collect both straight-grained lumber and pieces with the more unusual grain patterns often found around knots (Illus. 1-6). The straight grains have a "sobering" effect on the overall appearance of an intarsia composition, calling attention to the areas cut from curly grained wood.

A composition can be monotonous if every piece in it has only straight grains, and it can appear overly busy if every piece contains curly or unusual grains. Aim for a balance, playing up unusual grains by contrasting them with straight grains.

Knots are a natural occurrence in wood, and I believe there is nothing wrong with incorporating them into a design. Simply be sure the knot is

Illus. 1-5. To create visual interest, the grain direction was varied in the parts making up the central panel of this intarsia composition. Note how the parts appear lighter or darker than each other depending on the direction in which the grain is running.

Illus. 1-6. Compared with the straight grains generally found in knot-free wood, the grain patterns around knots can be quite unusual. Use these patterns to add interest to intarsia projects.

not loose in the board, and plan its placement so that it will not detract from the overall composition.

Summary of Wood Selection Sequence

1. Select the species of wood you prefer or can find locally.
2. Purchase wood of a nominal 1" (really 3/4") thickness and as wide as possible (to 12" wide).
3. Collect at least three or four shades of wood.
4. Look for boards that show gradual within-board color variations.
5. Collect both straight-grained and curly grained lumber.

Chapter 2

Lumber Drying

Lumber Drying

Drying the wood you use for intarsia properly is just as important as selecting it well. As noted in Chapter 1, we prefer to buy our wood wet, rather than kiln-dried, and then to dry it ourselves.

Generally, wet or damp lumber does not cause problems when you're sawing and assembling an intarsia project. Its effects show up only after the project is finished and on display. When, a year or so after we'd finished them, I looked at some of the first projects Judy and I had created together, I couldn't understand what had happened to the fit of the parts. I was sure I had done a better job of fit and finish than what I was seeing.

It took us some time to identify the problem: wet wood. When we first began to do intarsia together, the excitement of beginning each new project tended to override logical judgment. Even if we had realized the extent of the problems that moisture in the wood could cause, it probably wouldn't have held us back at that time.

And, after all, our wood "felt" dry. But "feeling" dry is just not good enough.

I'm not an authority on drying all species of wood; different woods require different drying times. But I can give you some tips on drying Western red cedar, our wood of choice.

Board Position

We prefer to stand our lumber upright, leaning against a wall, to dry. This lets us see the boards individually, as well as as a group, and helps us begin thinking about what projects specific boards might be used for.

If you are cramped for space, you can stack your lumber flat, placings stickers (little blocks of wood) between the boards. One drawback to this approach is that, while the wood is drying, you can see only the top board in each pile. It puts your visual dreaming on hold for a while.

The only "rule" I follow for positioning the lumber against the wall is not to lean more than one board against any spot.

The only "rule" I follow for positioning the lumber against the wall is not to lean more than one board against any spot. (Do not place two or more boards on top of one another). I also leave a space of 1" (or more) between the boards to increase air circulation and to give myself a place to grab hold of the board when I need to do so.

Board Identification

It's a good idea to use a lumber crayon to mark the color of the board on its face and to date the board with the month and year of purchase (Illus. 2-1). Marking the color helps you identify it accurately after the wood has dried and changed color slightly. The date identifies wood purchased on a single day should it get separated during drying or if you dry your lumber in more than one location. (You may have planned to use all the pieces you bought during a particular trip to the lumberyard in a single project.)

Illus. 2-1. For efficient drying, lean wet lumber against a wall in a single row. Mark lumber color and date of purchase on each board with a lumber crayon for later reference.

Rotating the Wood

As soon as you bring your newly purchased wet lumber home, the drying process starts. It is critical—during the first few days up to the first week of drying—to keep an close eye on the condition of newly purchased wet lumber, especially 1" x 12" material. Depending on how wet it is, the wood can begin to "cup" within the first few hours. When a board first starts to cup, immediately rotate it—that is, turn the side of the board facing the wall toward the open room.

Check each board every few hours—and rotate only those boards that have started to cup. Keep checking the wood and rotating it as needed. The goal is to keep the wood as flat as possible (Illus. 2-2).

The cupping slows as the lumber dries (after about the first week), and you should be able to rotate all the boards at the same time. However, it's still a good idea to check the pieces individually on a regular schedule and to rotate the ones that need it. If you allow the lumber to cup too far in one direction, it is very difficult, if not impossible, to remove the cup by rotating the wood. Even planing the wood when it is dry will not necessarily remove the cup.

When the cupping appears to have stopped, begin to rotate the lumber on a regular but less frequent basis (once a day works well) to ensure equal drying.

I use the same procedure to dry 2" thick wood as for 1" boards. The thicker material does not cup as fast as the 1" material, however, so it requires less frequent turning. I still rotate 2" boards on a regular basis to ensure that both sides dry equally.

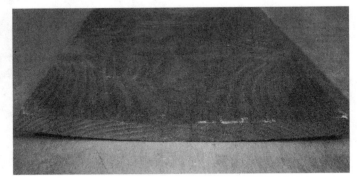

Illus. 2-2. A properly dried board is perfectly flat, like the one in the top photograph. The board at the bottom has cupped so badly that even planing will not remove the cup.

Dealing with Splits

You may buy wet boards that have splits on the ends. As soon as you get the wood home, trim off the ends of these boards at least several inches beyond the end of the split. Use a crayon to mark both sides of the board where the split would be had it continued. When you're ready to use the board, the crayon marks will tell you that there was a split in that area so that you can carefully inspect the board to see if the split continued as the board dried. If you detect a continuing split after the board is dry, mark its path with a crayon and then stay at least 1" away from the split on both sides when laying out your pattern pieces.

Some boards will continue to split even after you trim their ends. You can try trimming the end again, but some boards will continue to split no matter what you do to them. If that's the case, just let the board split and salvage what you can of it. Dark-colored WRC has more of a tendency to split than do the lighter colors.

Drying Time

Drying time depends on the moisture content in the purchased wood. The environment in which you store your lumber—especially its humidity—also affects drying time. In our studio (which is heated and cooled), it normally takes from 4 to 6 weeks to dry 1" x 12" material thoroughly. It can take as long as 6 months to dry 2" thick stock.

I've tried two approaches to speed the drying time—and I don't recommend either of them. The first is using a fan to circulate air around the lumber. This speeds up drying—but it also accelerates the speed with which the boards cup. Using a fan, the wood can begin to cup in 15 minutes or less, meaning it is ready to be rotated. You'll get little else done but watching and rotating your new lumber. And letting a fan run unattended overnight can create a disaster. Your boards may cup so badly by the next morning that there's no way to salvage them.

I have also placed boards in the hot sun to speed up the drying process. This also increased cupping, twisting, and warping. For me, drying in the sun is a definite "no."

When Is It Dry? And How Dry Is It?

In the early days, I devised several methods for determining when my lumber was dry. Unfortunately none of them was more than 50 percent accurate. The only sure-fire way of knowing that your lumber is dry—short of just letting it sit for 6 months—is to invest in a hand-held moisture meter in the back of this book.

I routinely use a moisture meter in our studio and have yet to be disappointed with the results. You can purchase this jewel for about $150—and it surely makes your life a lot easier. It's a tool well worth stretching the budget for!

At what moisture content your lumber is "dry" depends on the area of the country you live in. My moisture meter came with tables and charts for determining what "dry" is. After reading the instructions, I began testing the moisture content of every piece of wood in sight: old 2x4s, tabletops, newly purchased WRC, and WRC that had been lying around for years. Not only was all this testing interesting, but it let me know exactly what "dry" was in our studio.

Caution: To take a reading with a moisture meter, you use a probe. It is best not to probe the face of your intarsia boards because probing puts two little puncture wounds in the wood. These wounds close, making them invisible to the eye, but they reappear as "fang" marks after you have sanded and applied finish to the wood. I take the preliminary reading by probing the edge of the board. For the final reading, I cut the board in half about midway down its length and probe the end grain in several places (Illus. 2-3).

Illus. 2-3. A moisture meter is the only accurate way to know when lumber is dry. Probe the end of the board, not the face, to avoid making small puncture marks in wood that might show up on the face of your intarsia project.

Summary of Lumber Drying Sequence

1. Lean wet lumber against a wall in a single row.
2. Mark the color and the date of purchase on each board with a lumber crayon.
3. Regularly check each board for cup and rotate the boards as needed. (This is particularly critical in the first few days after purchase.)
4. Check with a moisture meter (or other method) for dryness.

Materials List

1. 1" x 12" (or 2" x 12") lumber
2. Lumber crayon, for marking wood color and date of purchase on boards
3. Moisture meter (optional), for determining when lumber is "dry"

Chapter 3

Layout

Layout

Now that your lumber is dry, you can start your first intarsia project.

Step 1: Choosing a Pattern

The first thing you will need for any intarsia project is a pattern. If you are new to intarsia, I suggest you start with a commercial pattern. The Dolphins (Illus. 3-1) are an easy first project for anyone just beginning to experiment with intarsia.

As I design and draw an intarsia pattern, I think about a number of things. Among them are what wood colors would look best where, whether an area will be too fragile to cut, whether a piece will be too small to work with or too large to fit on standard lumber, how to break up the pattern into parts to take advantage of wood shadings. I draw a small-scale sketch of the pattern first and do some pencil-shading to see how it might look. As I'm sketching, I try to foresee any problems that might arise in executing the project. When I've worked through the idea at the small scale, I enlarge the sketch to a size that is comfortable to work with.

As you learn more about intarsia techniques and work with patterns drawn by others, you may wish to design your own patterns. When you begin, however, a good pattern makes it easier to produce a professional finished project.

Step 2: Enlarging the Pattern

There are several ways to enlarge a drawing or a commercial pattern to finished-project size.

Method 1: Grids

When I began to work with my father, he did the designing and I took his sketches and enlarged them to the size needed for the finished project. My father worked on large projects, most of them created for banks, restaurants, hotels, and office buildings. The average size of the finished pieces was about 4' by 8'. This is the method I used to enlarge my father's small sketches.

I first drew a grid over the sketch, making the grid squares, for example, 1/2" on each side. Then, on a separate plain sheet of paper, I drew another set of grids double, triple, or more the size of the original grids. For example, I might use a 2" square grid, with each 1/2" square equal to one of my 2" squares. Then, I copied the contents of each 1/2" grid box into a 2" square, one square at a time. This approach lets you maintain the proportions of the original much more accurately than if you tried to redraw the sketch freehand at a larger size.

Method 2: Opaque Projector

If you have an opaque projector, or access to one, here's an easier method. Simply project the small sketch onto plain paper pinned to a

Illus. 3-1. The Dolphins, a simple free-form intarsia project, uses only two shades of wood.

smooth wall and trace the sketch onto the paper. Remember: the greater the distance between the projector and the paper, the larger the sketch will be. If you know the dimensions you want your finished piece to have, mark the width (or the height) of the finished piece on the large paper before pinning it to the wall. Then adjust the projector until the sketch fills the space you have marked.

Method 3: Photocopier/Blueprint Maker

Some commercial blueprint copying concerns can enlarge drawings to whatever size you need. A cheaper approach is to use a photocopier with enlargement capabilities, dividing the sketch into sections, enlarging each section equally, and then taping the enlargements together.

To begin the Dolphins, enlarge the Dolphin Pattern from the pattern section using whichever method you choose. The pattern was designed for a finished project size of 20½" wide by 9¾" high. You will need to enlarge the pattern as indicated to produce that finished size.

After you've enlarged your drawing or pattern, make any changes you wish to it before copying it to tracing paper.

Step 3: Making the Final Pattern

All the intarsia patterns we offer are printed on an almost transparent vellum paper. (See appendix for a current list of patterns available from Roberts Studio.)

Each pattern piece shows my recommendations for grain direction (marked with arrows) and for wood color ("MD," for example, stands for "medium dark shade of wood"). The grain direction arrows are simply recommendations; feel free to experiment with what suits your eye.

To prepare your own final pattern from an enlarged drawing, you'll need tracing paper and a fine-point red felt-tipped pen. Tracing paper is sold by the roll at art supply stores or some office supply stores. I buy both 24" and 36" widths. Place a piece of tracing paper over your drawing and carefully trace all the outlines with the red pen. Copy the color codes and the grain direction arrows on each part of the pattern.

Making a Template

If you plan to make an intarsia project in any quantities (for example, 25 of the same project), you might consider making a hard template of your pattern. This is particularly useful if the pattern is simple, like the Dolphins. (If your project consists of 50 or more parts, however, a template can be almost as much work to complete as the intarsia project itself—and you have to keep track of all the template parts.) The template simplifies tracing the pattern onto the wood, can give you greater accuracy, and keeps your pattern from wearing out.

We have found the best material for templates to be clear Plexiglas (about 1/16" thick). The Plexiglas lets you see both wood color and wood grain clearly. Alternative choices for template material are plywood or even cardboard.

Another approach to making more than one copy of an intarsia project is to make multiple copies of your pattern. Cut out the individual pattern pieces and mist the back side of each piece with spray adhesive. Then stick the pieces to the wood.

Step 4: Selecting and Preparing the Wood

With your full-size pattern in hand, you're ready to select the wood you'll use and plan how to lay the pattern pieces out on it.

Note: If the intarsia project you have selected is a framed format, we have found that it's best to make the frame first, before transferring the pattern pieces to the wood. Measure the outside dimensions of the pattern and make the frame accordingly. When it is complete, measure its inside dimensions and then adjust the pattern lines so that they match the frame measurements exactly. I used to trace and cut out all the wood parts first and then try to make the frame fit the project. Invariably, the frame turned out just a little smaller than the wood parts. Believe me, it is no fun to trim all the edge parts so that the project fits inside the frame!

Before doing anything else, it's a good idea to take a little time to study your pattern and to prepare a plan of action. I note all the wood colors I'll need, check whether the pattern (like the Dolphins) calls for dowels that will need to be purchased, decide whether there are any pieces that should be cut from wood thinner than 3/4" and look for any areas that should be "stack-cut."

Picking Boards

Like all the patterns we offer, the Dolphins are designed to be cut from nominal 1" (3/4" thick) wood—because 3/4" thick wood is easier to find and to cut than is nominal 2" wood. If more dimension is desirable for a specific project, it's possible to raise a 3/4" thick part by inserting a shim under it. (The process will be explained in Chapter 6.) However, you can use wood of any thickness you desire.

For the Dolphins, you will need only two colors of wood: medium dark and white. Many intarsia projects use up to six different shades of wood, but the Dolphins are an easy "first" project.

Planing the Wood

WRC is generally sold "good," or sanded one side (S1S), but the good surface can still be rough. Plane about 1/16" (the least amount possible to make a smooth surface to trace onto) from the good side of the wood. If you don't have a planer, you might use a belt sander.

I usually plane my lumber only when I'm ready to work with it. The fresh cut soon changes color, making it difficult, without planing it again, to see its true color (Illus. 3-2). It's frustrating to be working with what you think is a medium-color wood and then to find out it is a light color after you start the shaping process—especially if you have a very good fit!

If the rough side of the wood is uneven, it's a good idea to smooth it out also so that the wood will lie flat when you are cutting it and when you glue the intarsia parts cut from it to the project backing.

Check the wood you have selected for any cracks or imperfections to avoid when you lay out your pattern pieces. If these are difficult to see, use a dark pen to circle them or draw on top of a hairline crack to make it more visible.

Planning for Thin Pieces

Some intarsia projects, especially those with a framed format, have what I call a background. These are the wood pieces that make up, for example, the sky or water that surrounds the main part of the design. I like to cut these parts from thinner wood—3/8" rather than 3/4" thick—than the main sections of the pattern. (We have had problems with warping and with cracks in large pieces when we planed WRC thinner than 3/8".) There are two ways to prepare to cut these thinner pieces.

If you have only a few small pieces to cut from thinner wood, trace these pattern pieces in one area of your 3/4" thick board, cut the section on which you've traced them long enough to fit in the planer, and then plane the back side to 3/8" thick. (Pay attention when you are doing this. Jerry and I have accidently planed the good side of the piece, with the pattern markings!) If you have large pieces or many small pieces that must be cut from 3/8" thick stock, plane the wood down to the 3/8" thickness before transferring the design to it.

If you don't have a planer, either resaw the wood or look for a cabinet shop that will plane some lumber for you.

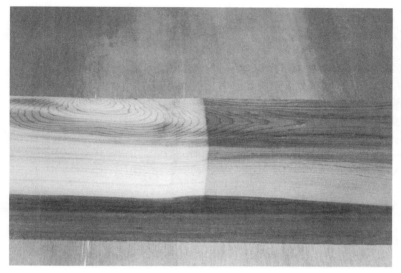

Illus. 3-2. After this board was planed, it sat around for a few months. Then the left side was planed again. Note how much the surface of the light-colored wood darkened while the board was in storage.

Planning a Stack-Cut

Although there are no parts like this in the Dolphins, this is the time to consider whether there are any parts in a pattern that should be stack-cut. To identify candidates for stack-cutting, look for adjoining parts of different colors with zig-zag outlines containing right angles—outlines it would be impossible to reach with a saw without damaging adjoining or surrounding parts. Your goal with stack-cutting is to trace and cut two identical copies of these adjoining parts, one from light wood and the other from dark, and then to cut the adjoining parts apart on the separating outline. You will then have one dark section that fits exactly with its adjoining light section—and two mirror-image parts you can discard.

When I stack-cut parts, I generally lay out and trace the parts (both the lighter and the darker parts) on the lighter of the two wood colors. Then I cut off most of the excess light wood around the parts, lay the light wood section on top of the darker wood, and use a pen to draw around the outline of the light section. I then cut the darker section on that outline and use double-sided tape to hold the two pieces of wood together while I saw the parts. After you've cut the parts out, remove the tape and match the appropriately colored parts. Wait until you are ready to saw the parts before applying the tape, and remove it as soon as possible after you have cut them. If you leave the tape on overnight, it can be almost impossible to separate the two pieces of wood.

Step 5: Laying Out the Pattern Pieces

Layout is the process of determining which pattern pieces to cut from which sections of the wood you've selected. To lay out your pattern pieces, start with one shade of wood. There is no "best" shade to begin with. It's really up to you.

For the Dolphins, we'll start with the medium dark shade because most of the parts are cut from that wood color. First lay out and trace all the medium dark parts; then lay out and trace all the white parts.

Layout is one of the most creative aspects of intarsia. Think about how you can make the most of the pieces of wood you're using. Figure out where each important pattern piece might go before you start to trace any of the parts onto the wood.

Position the pattern on the face of the wood, lining up the arrows on the pattern that show grain direction with the grain direction on the piece of wood you are using (Illus. 3-3). This is where having your pattern on transparent paper is so handy. As you move the pattern around, you can see the grain and the color differences in the wood underneath. Since intarsia relies heavily on wood color and wood grain patterns for its impact, selecting just the right wood area for a part can make or break a project. Work with your pattern, moving it around to various areas of your board.

The simplicity of the Dolphins lends itself to the use of curly or unusual wood grains. Experiment with your pattern. Keep the table you work on clean and uncluttered so that you can move your pattern around without its getting hung up on anything (like a coffee cup). It's also important to keep your pattern free of folds, wrinkles, and moisture. The overall accuracy of your project—how well your parts fit together after they are sawn—depends on the integrity of your pattern.

Board ends are prone to splitting. Ends that do not have obvious splits can have hairline cracks that the eye cannot see. Because of this, it's wise to stay a few inches away from the ends of the board when you lay out your pattern pieces.

Be sure to leave some space between pattern pieces that are not adjoining parts. Like many people, I want to waste as little wood as possible so I position the parts closer together than I should, making it very difficult to cut the board up into workable sections. Especially when you're beginning, give yourself plenty of room between parts.

Adjoining parts that have the same grain direction and are the same color are an exception to this rule. Such parts should be traced as one piece, without space between them, and then cut apart during sawing. For the Dolphins, for example, lay out each dolphin with its flipper and its dorsal fin attached (Illus. 3-4). Use this technique whenever you can. It ensures a good fit between parts.

When you've figured out where you want to cut your parts from the wood you've chosen, position your pattern for the first part and put some pushpins at the corners of the pattern to hold it in place. Now you're ready to trace your first part onto the wood.

Step 6: Transferring the Pattern to the Wood

There are several ways to transfer a design to wood. I find the easiest is to use a fine ballpoint pen with black or blue ink and legal-size (8 ½" x 14")

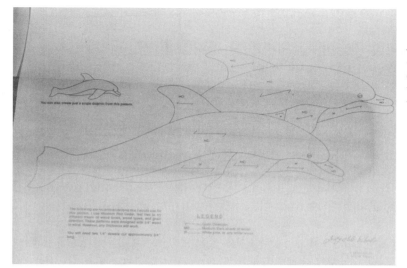

Illus. 3-3. Preparing the final pattern on a nearly transparent paper (like tracing paper) lets you see the wood grain and color variations when you lay out your project.

Illus. 3-4. Adjoining parts that have the same grain direction and wood color markings on the pattern should be transferred to the wood as one piece and then cut apart later. This approach improves fit.

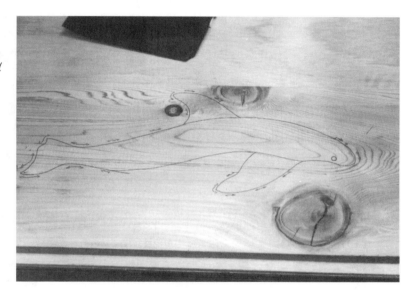

pen-and-pencil carbon paper. (A box of 100 sheets from an office supply store usually lasts me a year.) After I've used a sheet two or three times, I give it a good dusting with a foxtail brush. This removes the sawdust that sticks to the carbon side and makes it almost as good as new.

You can generally spot an intarsia buff by the ink blobs on the undersides of his or her hands and arms. A fellow called me recently to ask what kind of pen I use to transfer my patterns to wood because ink from his pen was getting all over his arm and the pattern. I had to laugh because I had thought that only happened to me! (I think that the sawdust is the cause of all this. The ink sticks to the little blobs of dust and the next thing you know they are on your arm.) Jerry has a good laugh when I end up with ink all over my face. A warning: don't wear a "good" long-sleeve shirt while laying out and tracing your pattern.

Slide one or more sheets of carbon paper under the part of the pattern you are ready to trace, smooth the pattern out, and put more pushpins around the outside of the part you have laid out, to hold it in place as you trace around it (Illus. 3-5). If possible, keep the pushpins to the outer edges of the board. Otherwise, you may end up with a pushpin hole right in the middle of one of your intarsia parts. If I've made a lot of pushpin holes that I want to avoid, I'll draw a circle around each one with a pen.

I've found that tracing freehand works best. When tracing a curved area, keep your hand inside the curve. This makes your hand work like a compass (Illus. 3-6). Some people use French curves or circle templates in tracing. These may be a help for certain patterns.

As I trace my pattern, I use some special markings to give myself more information. If, like the Dolphins, the project has a "free-form" format (no background or frame), I mark the exposed outer edges of the parts with arrows to indicate that no parts fit next to these edges. When you begin to saw your parts, you'll know that you can relax a bit in these areas. I draw one line perpendicular to the arrow to show where to start relaxing and another line to show where to stop (Illus. 3-7).

Extending the pattern lines beyond the actual part or giving yourself a "lead" line by continuing the outline as though you were starting to draw the adjoining part are two helpful tracing techniques (Illus. 3-8). These extended lines give you time to line up your saw blade before you reach the "good" section of the cut.

If, as you trace your pattern, your pen drifts off the line and you correct it, you may end up with a very heavy line. By the time you're ready to cut that part, you may not remember which side of the line is the correct one. When this happens, draw an arrow to the side of the line to follow (Illus. 3-9). Also keep in mind that if you do drift off the line as you trace, you may not need to correct it if there is no adjoining part or if you simply follow your "inaccurate" line when you draw the outline of the adjoining part.

It takes time and practice to develop skill in laying out pattern pieces and tracing outlines. Be easy on yourself as you work on your first project.

As I trace each pattern part, I give it a number. (When you write the number on the pattern, the carbon paper transfers it to the wood.) In this way, the pattern becomes a map to follow when it's time to put the project together. Numbering parts is especially helpful when you have 100 or more in a project. Numbering is optional on the Dolphins because there are so few parts.

It's important, when you finish tracing a part, to check to see that you have copied its entire outline. (After you've used a pattern a few times, it can be difficult to see which lines you have traced.) After tracing each part, remove only enough pushpins to check the traced outline (Illus. 3-10). If you remove all your pushpins and then discover that

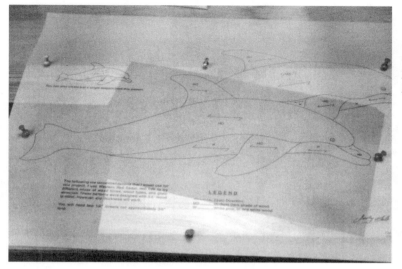

Illus. 3-5. Hold the pattern and the carbon paper firmly in place with pushpins when tracing the pattern pieces onto the wood.

Illus. 3-6. Left: Holding your pen inside the radius of a curve makes it easier to trace a smooth curve. Right: It's much more difficult to trace a curve accurately from the outside.

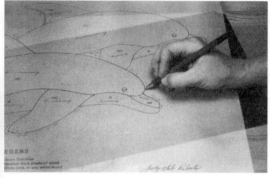

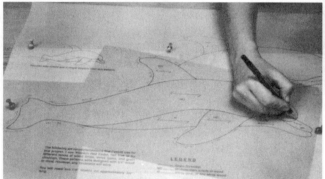

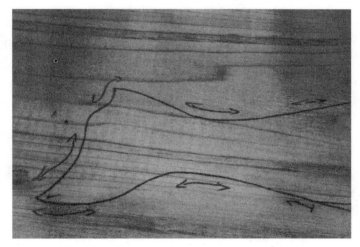

Illus. 3-7. When tracing a pattern, use arrows to mark areas that do not have adjoining parts. The arrows let you know that you can relax a bit when sawing these outlines.

Illus. 3-10. *Extending a pattern outline beyond the actual part, as though you were beginning to draw the adjoining part, provides a "lead" on which to line up the saw blade.*

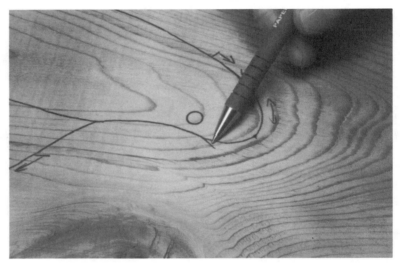

Illus. 3-11. *Mark the "good" line—the one on which to cut—with arrows if you drift off the pattern outline as you trace it.*

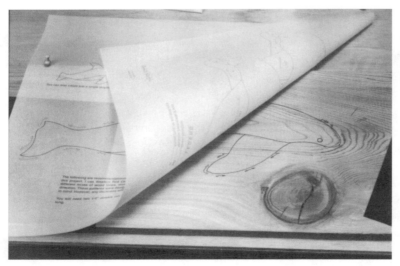

Illus. 3-12. *Check each part as you trace it to see that you've transferred the entire outline. Remove only enough pushpins to reveal the outline.*

you've forgotten to trace a segment of the outline, it can be difficult to reposition the pattern in the exact same spot to complete the outline.

When you've finished laying out and tracing every part for the Dolphins—first the medium dark and then the light parts—you're ready to begin sawing.

Summary of Layout Sequence

1. Enlarge the pattern. Use grids, an opaque projector, or a photocopier.

2. Copy the pattern onto tracing paper, using a red felt-tipped pen. Also copy the grain direction arrows and the wood colors.

3. Pick out the wood. Clean/plane the surface so that it is easy to trace onto.

4. Place the pattern on the wood, following the grain direction arrows. Use pushpins to keep the pattern in place.

5. Slide carbon paper under the section of the pattern you want to transfer to the wood.

6. Smooth out the pattern and the carbon paper, using more pushpins to hold them in place.

7. Transfer all the pattern part outlines to the wood, numbering the parts as you do so.

8. Where appropriate, prepare parts for stack-cutting. Lay out the parts on the lighter of the two woods. Plan to use double-sided tape to hold the two wood colors together when you're ready to cut.

Materials List for Dolphins

1. Fine-point red felt-tipped pen, for making the pattern

2. Tracing paper (at least 23" x 11" or tape smaller pieces together), for making the pattern

3. Two shades of wood (medium dark and white), for the project

4. Fine-point blue or black ballpoint pen, for layout

5. Pen-and-pencil legal-size (8½" x 14") carbon paper, for layout

6. Pushpins, for layout

Chapter 4

Sawing

Sawing

Sawing is both challenging and rewarding, and it may be the single most important and demanding step in intarsia. Unlike many of the other steps, sawing is "final." Although it's sometimes possible to trim an ill-fitting part, trimming can cause gaps and spaces elsewhere in the project.

Over the years, I've spent some time analyzing the activity of sawing. I've tried to pin problems on all kinds of things, but most of the time the real source is the operator. Any saw has its limitations. The most critical one is generally the operator's skill with it.

In this chapter, I'll share my experience with the saws I use to cut intarsia—and offer some sawing tips I've learned over time.

Selecting a Saw for Intarsia

The two most flexible power saws—and those best suited to intarsia—are the band saw and the scroll saw. Which to use is a matter of personal choice. You can successfully cut intarsia projects with either one. The two saws complement each other nicely, however. If you have one of each, you can fit the saw to the type of cut you're making.

You can also cut intarsia with a hand saw (for example, a coping saw) or with a jigsaw or a saber saw, but most people prefer the ease and accuracy of a band and/or a scroll saw.

If you are new to woodworking and do not own a power saw, do your homework before deciding which saw to buy. Read articles in woodworking magazines, and look for books on saws at your local library.

If you are lucky enough to have a woodworking show in your area, the dealers exhibiting there will be eager to answer your questions and to let you try out their machines. If possible, pick a dealer who will let you "try before you buy"—or at least make sure the dealer has a money-back guarantee, in case you are not satisfied with the saw.

My primary intarsia saw is a band saw; I also use a scroll saw for some types of work. If you are purchasing only one saw and want it to serve for many different types of craft projects, however, a scroll saw may be a more versatile choice than a band saw.

Band Saw

The configuration of a band saw (Illus. 4-1) limits the width or turning radius of the piece you can handle to the measurement between the band saw blade and the saw column. This is called the saw's throat capacity. A band saw puts no limit on the length of piece you can cut.

The most popular band saw sizes are the 10" and 12" models (those with a 10" or 12" throat capacity). From there, band saw sizes range upward in 2" increments: 14", 16" and so on.

If you are purchasing a band saw specifically for intarsia, a 12" is the minimum size I would recommend. The most popular band saw on the

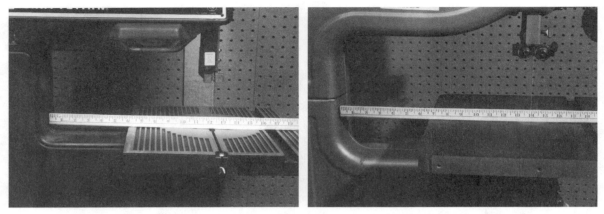

Illus. 4-1. A band saw with a 12" (left) or a 14" (right) throat capacity is a good choice for intarsia work. The 12" model has the standard steel block guides installed; the 14" saw is equipped with roller guides.

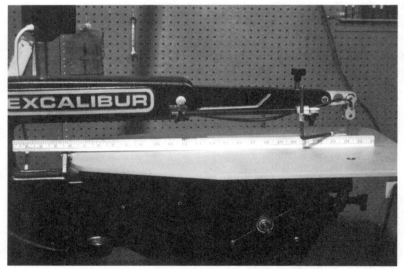

Illus. 4-2. This 24" scroll saw should accommodate almost any intarsia project.

market today may be the Sears 12 "model. It's a good starter for those on a limited budget. If your budget permits, however, and you want a saw that places the fewest limitations on potential projects, a 14" model is preferable. I used a Sears 12" model (before the tilting head versions were available) for years before graduating to a 14" model. (If you already own a 10" band saw, go ahead and use it. You'll simply encounter more limitations than with a larger saw.)

Scroll Saw

A scroll saw (Illus. 4-2) limits the length of the wood you can handle, but not the width of the piece.

Scroll saw models ranging in size from 14" to 24" are the most popular, with various manufacturers offering different size ranges. Scroll saws of the same size can differ greatly in price, also depending on the manufacturer.

A 14" scroll saw is adequate for most intarsia projects, but for me, bigger is better. We use a 24" model and have encountered no size limitations. A scroll saw with a variable speed setting is very useful.

A scroll saw's rate of cut is somewhat slower than a band saw's when sawing 3/4" stock, and it is substantially slower when sawing material more than 1" thick. Since speed of cutting is not really important for intarsia, however, the slower cutting speed of the scroll saw makes little or no difference in the choice of a saw for this craft.

Tips for Outfitting a Band Saw

Since I cut most of my intarsia work with a band saw, the instructions and tips that follow feature its use. As mentioned earlier, however, it is not the only saw suitable for intarsia. Except for the fact that a scroll saw has no blade guides, I successfully use the same sawing techniques with my scroll saw.

Choosing Band Saw Blade Guides

Steel Block Guides. Most band saws sold today have two sets of solid steel blade guides: one set above the table; the other set, below the table. Both sets of blade guides also have a roller bearing behind the blade. To set up a saw with guides of this type, follow the recommendations in the owner's manual supplied with the saw. The steel blade guides do a good job of keeping the saw running straight. They can, however, cause the blade to overheat, especially if you set them a little too tight against the blade.

Resin Block Guides. Especially if you are using a 1/16" or a 1/8" wide blade, consider replacing the steel guides with an after-market set of guides made of a resin compound impregnated with graphite (Illus. 4-3). You can place these composite blade guides much closer to the blade without causing the blade to heat up. Placing the blade guides close to the blade reduces blade twisting, providing better saw control. The graphite-impregnated guide blocks do, however, wear faster than steel ones and have to be rotated to a fresh side periodically. They can be refaced easily when all usable sides are worn. I highly recommend these guides. (For a supply source, see the Buyer's Guide.)

Roller Guides. My favorite band saw guides, however, are roller guides (Illus. 4-4). Roller guides provide the best of both worlds because they remain cool during operation yet have a long lifespan. These also have the standard roller in back of the blade.

Choosing a Band Saw Blade

Blade Width. If you are just starting out with intarsia, have only one band saw, and do not wish to change blades, I recommend using a 1/8" wide blade for all your cuts.

In our studio, we keep two band saws set up. One has a 1/8" blade, which allows sharp turns. On the other, we use a 1/4" blade, which cuts large, smooth curves and straight lines with less drifting from side to side.

Some intarsia enthusiasts swear by a 1/16" blade. Use whatever blade width you are comfortable with. It's really a matter of personal choice.

Blade Type and Quality. With my original 12" Sears band saw, I used a standard (nonpremium) Sears wood-cutting blade. This blade cut our soft WRC very nicely. I have tried premium blades; they are extremely sharp, offer no resistance, cut very fast, and last five to ten times longer than the standard blades. The problem is that these blades are "too good" for intarsia. The premium blades cut so fast that I had no control. For intarsia, a blade that offers some degree of resistance when the material is fed into it provides better control. (There is a fine line between resistance and just

"If you are just starting out with intarsia, have only one band saw, and do not wish to change blades, I recommend using a 1/8" wide blade for all your cuts."

Illus. 4-3. Block-type blade guides made from graphite-impregnated resin can be adjusted closer to the band saw blade than steel guides without causing the blade to overheat. Note: Upper blade guard removed for photography.

plain "dull," however.) Because the Sears standard blade is also thinner than the premium blade, it has a smaller kerf (the width of the cut made by the saw blade).

I recommend that you start with a 1/8" x 15-tooth or a 1/4" x 6-tooth blade. Sears stores stock the standard wood-cutting blades for the 12" band saw. Standard blades for the 14" band model must be ordered from the Sears catalog in the back of this book.

Illus. 4-4. Roller blade guides keep the band saw blade running straight. Note: Upper blade guard removed for photography.

Padding the Band Saw Table

If your band saw has a grooved table (like the 12" Sears Craftsman model in Illus. 4-5), I encourage you to make a pad to cover the table. The reason? When you make any cut, the saw blade creates a burr on the underside of the wood, and this burr tends to hang up on the grooves in the table. When you use a band saw only for straight cuts (so that the burr runs in the direction of the grooves), the burr generally does not cause any problems. In intarsia, however, most cuts are curved, and the burr hangs up on the grooves as it crosses over them. This is frustrating—and it can be dangerous. There's no way to know if the piece is really hung up (hitting something solid) or just resisting feeding because of the burr.

To eliminate this nuisance, I constructed a pad to cover the grooved top of my band saw table. To make a pad like mine, use a very flat piece of good-quality 1/4" plywood a bit bigger than the dimensions of your saw table.

Measure the width of the saw table and its distance from front to back. Then cut a blank from the plywood about the same width as the saw table and a couple of inches longer than the dimension from front to back. Measure the width of the slot that the miter gauge fits in and cut a piece of plywood that will just slip into that slot and is as long as the front-to-back dimension of the table. Cut two more pieces of about the same width, but with lengths equal to the width of the saw table (Illus. 4-6).

Measure from the left edge of the saw table to the center of the saw blade. Using that measurement, mark a line on the plywood pad to indicate where to cut the blade clearance slot. Also measure from the front of the table to the back of the blade. Add 1" to that measurement and mark it on the blade clearance slot line on the pad. (Remember, the pad is about 2" longer than the front-to-back table dimension; you add 1" to the blade clearance slot so that the pad will hang over the front of the table 1"). Now cut the blade clearance slot 1/16" to 1/8" wide.

Illus. 4-6. The underside of this pad for covering a grooved band saw table shows how it's constructed. The horizontal wood strips fit against the outside front and back edges of the saw table and hold the pad securely in place. The vertical wood strip slips into the table's miter slot. Note the clearance slot for the saw blade.

With the saw turned OFF, slide the pad onto the table from the back, placing the saw blade in the blade clearance slot. Center the pad from front to back, keeping the blade in the center of the slot. (If the slot doesn't fit the blade properly, correct the problem now.) When the pad fits properly, mark the location of the miter slot on the underside of the pad. (Be sure to mark its width and its length at both the front and back edges of the pad.)

Remove the pad from the saw table, turn it over, and fasten the miter slot strip you cut earlier to the underside of the pad. (Use some glue in addition to nails or other fasteners.) Turn the pad over and slide it back on the table to check the position of the miter slot strip.

If the fit is good, mark the location of the outside front and back edges of the saw table on the underside of the pad. Remove the pad, turn it over again, position one of the strips you cut earlier at the front of the pad, and mark where it intersects the saw blade clearance slot. Cut the strip on that mark and then attach the two sections (one on either side of the blade clearance slot) to the front of the pad. Note: Install the front and back strips 1/16" to 1/8" away from the line for the outside table edge. This clearance lets you remove the pad from the table more easily.

With the front strip in place, put the pad back on the saw table and check (and correct if necessary) your earlier positioning mark for the strip at the rear of the table. Fasten the rear strip to the pad—and you have a smooth band saw table top!

Intarsia Sawing Tips and Techniques

Since sawing can at times take many hours, I prefer to sit at my band saw. I also keep at my side a few small tools that I use constantly while cutting out a project. Although these tools may seem simple, they play a vital role in the final outcome of my sawing. They are shown in Illus. 4-7. I'll explain their use throughout this section:

- Good-quality 6" square
- Sanding block with coarse sandpaper
- Round plug as a gauge for curves

Checking the Saw for Squareness

Before beginning to saw a project, always set your saw and check it for squareness by making test cuts and checking them. If you've set your saw up properly, you'll find that most out-of-squareness conditions are due to operator error. As I saw, I constantly check my parts for squareness with a good-quality 6" square (Illus. 4-8).

Illus. 4-7. These simple tools help you saw high-quality intarsia parts. Use the 6" square to check the squareness of your work, the sanding block to remove burrs from the underside of the wood, and the round plugs to determine whether your saw will cut specific curves. The diameter of the plug you use should correspond with the thickness of your saw blade: a 1/2" diameter plug for a 1/8" thick blade and a 1½" diameter for a 1/4" blade.

Illus. 4-8. As you cut intarsia parts, monitor your sawing technique by checking the parts regularly with a good-quality square like this 6" one.

Preventing Out-of-Square Parts

Aside from not following the layout line, a major reason for ill-fitting intarsia parts is out-of-squareness of the parts. The thicker the wood you are using, the more out-of-squareness affects the fit of the parts. A few precautionary measures will minimize this problem.

Remove Burrs. As you make a cut, the saw blade forms a burr (rough wood) between the wood piece and the saw table. This burr keeps the wood from lying flat on the table. If the wood rocks or tilts slightly before it contacts the saw blade, the blade may cut the part out of square or inaccurately. Working with wood that lies flat on the saw table eliminates one negative factor to contend with in cutting accurate parts.

Before beginning to saw a part from any piece of wood that has been cut before, remove the burr on the underside of the piece. Keep a sanding block handy for this purpose. I use a block made from a piece of scrap (Illus. 4-9). It's about 2¼" wide by 9½" long by 1½" thick. (As long as the block fits your hand comfortably, its exact dimensions are not impor-

Illus. 4-9. An emery-covered sanding block is essential to accurate intarsia saw work.

tant.) I wrap a piece of coarse emery cloth around the bottom and up the two narrow ends of the block, stapling the cloth in place on the ends.

Get into the habit of sanding the burr off the back side of the wood each time you complete a cut. Illus. 4-10 shows the burr on two pieces of wood that have just been cut apart; it also illustrates the result of sanding.

Adjust Blade Guides Properly. A second cause of out-of-squareness is adjusting the top saw blade guides too high over the wood. Most owner's manuals advise setting the guides as close to the material being cut as possible without their touching the wood. Sawing intarsia is an exception to that rule. I adjust the blade guides far enough above the wood to allow clearance for my fingers to pass under the guides. (I try not to get my fingers too close to the blade, but at times it can't be helped.)

I mentioned earlier the importance of setting the left and right blade guides close to the blade—to keep the blade running straight. Keeping the blade from twisting is very important in preventing out-of-square parts.

Use Correct Feeding Techniques. In operating a band saw, the object is to put the center of the blade on the center of the layout line (Illus. 4-11). When you follow this rule, the saw cut removes all traces of the layout line. As I saw, I constantly remind myself to feed the wood directly into the face of the blade. If, while sawing, my concentration lapses, I tend to feed slightly to the right (or left) side of the blade, rather than straight into its face. This causes my parts to be out of square.

Illus. 4-10. Above: The saw blade forms burrs like these each time it makes a cut. Right: A sanding block removes the burrs from the pieces before resawing so they will lie flat on the saw table.

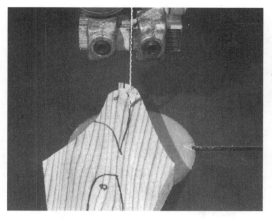

Illus. 4-11. Feed the wood straight into the face of the saw blade. The cut should eliminate the layout line.

When band-sawing curved lines, remember that the saw blade makes straight cuts only; the operator cuts the curves. To cut an accurate curve, you—the operator—must be completely in control of the feeding of the part.

Since I'm right-handed, I try to keep the part on the right side of the blade, with the waste to the left side of the blade. Although this position is not always possible, it is the natural way for me to saw.

Cutting Boards into Blanks

Before beginning to saw individual parts, cut your boards into blanks (pieces) that are easy to handle and that, if possible, do not exceed the maximum dimensions of your saw. Clean the burr from the underside of each blank.

Marking Adjoining Parts

If you laid out adjoining parts without space between them (as recommended in Chapter 3), use a pencil to draw two short lines across the layout line separating the parts before sawing them apart. When you assemble the project later, simply match the lines to position the parts exactly as the pattern calls for.

Planning the Saw Path

Before you put your saw to any wood, plot out your saw path. Think about the best place to start and end each cut, looking for potential trouble spots. Measure any large parts to determine whether they will fit within the throat capacity of your saw. If you are using a band saw, the limitation will likely be 14" or less. Parts wider than your saw's throat capacity can most likely be sawn along their length. Plan where to begin and end your cut accordingly.

Checking Curve Before Cutting Them

To check a curve on an intarsia part to determine whether you can cut it with the blade width you are using, make a round plug gauge that corresponds with your saw blade width. If you are using a 1/8" blade, you want a 1/2" diameter plug. (A 1/2" dowel works perfectly.) If you are using a 1/4" blade, you need a plug with a 1½" diameter (Illus. 4-12). If your plug is larger than the curve and it's an inside curve, you'll need a narrower saw blade to cut it.

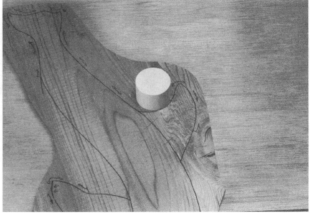

*Illus. 4-12. For a band saw running a 1/4"
wide blade, use a 1½" diameter plug to
check an inside curve like this one before
sawing it. If the gauge is equal to or
smaller than the curve, as it is here, the
saw can cut the curve.*

Inside Curves. When cutting an inside curve (radius), the saw blade
can enter and exit the curve on the layout line only if the curve is the
same size or larger than your plug gauge. If your plug gauge does not fit a
tight curve, the saw blade will not stay on the cutting line as you make the
turn. A too-wide blade will run "wide" on an inside curve, cutting into the
good wood of the part and creating an excessive "gap" if another part fits
into the curve.

Outside Curves. If, on the other hand, the part has a tight outside curve
(radius), the saw blade will be able to make that turn even though the
curve is smaller than your gauge—with preplanning.

*Illus. 4-13. Above: Checking this outside
curve with a gauge shows that it is smaller
than the minimum turning radius of the saw.
To cut a curve like this one, use the peeling
technique. Center: First cut relief slots
around the curve. Keep them at least 1/16"
from the sawing line. Far right: As you saw
the curve, the excess wood straightens up
and "peels" off the curve much like the skin
of an orange.*

To cut an outside curve smaller than your plug, first cut relief slots all the way around the tight curve. The slots should be at least 1/16" apart and should extend no closer to the layout line than 1/16".

To cut the part, begin sawing where you normally would, slowing the rate of feed as you reach the tight curve. The waste material in which you sawed the relief slots will start to straighten out as it is cut away and will not hit the back of the saw blade. I call this technique peeling because when the relief-cut wood begins to straighten out, it reminds me of peeling an orange. The peeling process is shown in Illus. 4-13.

Dealing with Errors

If, as you saw your parts, you should drift slightly off the layout line, don't try to do anything about it while you're sawing. It's best to complete all the sawing, assemble all the parts and check them for fit, and then do any trimming that is necessary. (Trimming and shaping are discussed in Chapters 5 and 6.)

Drill Before Sawing

Check the pattern for any parts with holes that need to be drilled and take care of that operation before you begin to saw.

Step-by-Step Sawing Guide for the Dolphins

The instructions that follow assume that you are cutting the Dolphins with a band saw. The band saw in the photographs has a 14" throat capacity and is equipped with a 1/8" wide blade.

Step 1: Cut Blanks

Cut the boards on which you laid out the Dolphins into five blanks. As shown in Illus. 4-14, you'll have three dark blanks (one for each dolphin's body and one containing the noses of both dolphins) and two white blanks.

Illus. 4-14. Before sawing any parts, cut the boards for the Dolphins into manageable blanks.

Step 2: Remove Burrs

Remove the burrs from the back of each blank with a sanding block (Illus. 4-15).

Illus. 4-15. Deburr the underside of every cut piece so it will lie flat on the saw table

Step 3: Drill Holes

Drill a 1/4" hole in each dolphin for the eye (Illus. 4-16).

Illus. 4-16. Before sawing, drill a hole in each body for the dolphin's eye.

Step 4: Mark Adjoining Pieces

If you laid out the Dolphins as Judy suggested in Chapter 3, you traced the dorsal fin above each dolphin's body and the flipper below it as one piece with the dolphin's body. Before beginning to saw, make two pencil marks across the layout line separating the fin from the body, and two lines across the layout line separating the flipper from the body (Illus. 4-17). These lines tell you exactly how to position the fin and the flipper when you are ready to assemble the parts.

Step 5: Check Curves

If you are using a 1/8" wide blade, check the radius of the curve at the dolphin's head with the 1/2" plug gauge, to ensure that you will be able to cut the curve without a problem (Illus. 4-18). As the photograph shows, if you are using a 1/4" blade (and therefore a 1½" plug gauge) you will not be able to make the turn. Plan to cut relief slots and use the peeling technique described earlier on the previous page.

Illus. 4-17. To aid positioning later, cross-mark the layout lines where the dorsal fin and the flipper join the dolphin body.

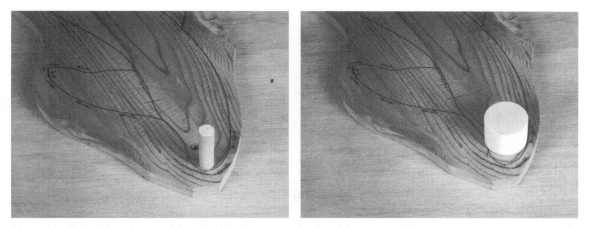

Illus. 4-18. Left: A band saw with a 1/8" blade can cut the outside curve of the dolphin's head without peeling. Right: Cut relief slots around the outside curve of the dolphin's head before trying to cut it with a 1/4" blade.

Step 6: Plan Your Saw Path

Measure the larger of the two dolphins across its widest part (from the end of the lower part of the tail to the tip of the head). If you enlarged the Dolphin Pattern as recommended in Chapter 3, the measurement should be about 17" (Illus. 4-19). If you are using a 14" or smaller band saw, this is a potential trouble spot—because 17" exceeds the throat capacity of your saw. If you begin to saw at the tip of the upper tail, move toward the head, make the turn around the tip of the head, and then saw back toward the lower tail, you will not have enough clearance between the blade and the saw column to complete the cut. However, if you start at the bottom tip of the tail and saw toward the head (Illus. 4-20), the part will swing outward, away from the column, when you reach the front of the head, allowing you to continue around the piece and all the way back to the upper tip of the tail.

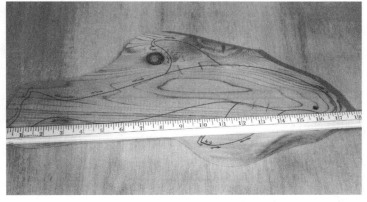

Illus. 4-19. At 17", the larger dolphin's body is wider than most band saw throat capacities.

Illus. 4-20. If a piece exceeds the saw's throat capacity, figure out where to start the cut so that the piece will swing away from the saw column as it is sawed.

Step 7: Saw Body of Larger Dolphin

Beginning with the larger of the two dolphin bodies, start at the lower tip of the tail and saw toward the head (as in Illus. 4-20).

When you reach the place where the rear of the white belly section joins the body, exit the part there (Illus. 4-21). In the photograph you can see the lead line Judy drew at that spot during layout. During sawing the lead line serves as a guide for exiting or entering the part. You'll get the best fit between parts by exiting the cut where another part adjoins the part you are cutting, rather than by trying to continue the cut on the layout line. This is because the line often makes a slight change of direction at these junctures, and it can be difficult to adjust the position of the wood so that the saw cuts exactly on the layout line.

After you exit the cut, use your sanding block to remove the burr on the underside of the tail section you just cut. Then return the piece to the saw table.

Continue the cut, beginning at the back of the belly section where you exited (Illus. 4-22). Be very careful in this area to keep the saw on the layout line because another part adjoins in this area. Continue sawing along the section of the layout line where the flipper adjoins the body (Illus. 4-23) and toward the head. Exit the cut where the nose part joins the body (Illus. 4-24), following the lead line you drew during layout. Remove the burr from the back of the piece.

Return the piece to the saw table and begin the cut (Illus. 4-25) where you exited. Continue sawing around the head (Illus. 4-26), along the upper back, through the section where the dorsal fin adjoins the body (Illus. 4-27), and to the end of the tail. At that point, exit the cut one last time (Illus. 4-28). Remove the burr from the back of the dolphin body, return the piece to the table, and cut the end of the tail.

As shown in Illus. 4-29, you've completed cutting the body of the larger dolphin; its dorsal fin and its flipper are still in blanks.

Step 8: Saw Dorsal Fin and Flipper of Larger Dolphin

Before cutting the dorsal fin, use your plug gauge (1/2" for a 1/8" blade) to check the tight rounded area of the fin to see if the blade will make the turn (Illus. 4-30). If you enlarged the pattern following Judy's recommendation, the tight radius will be smaller than the plug. That means you will need to cut relief slots (Illus. 4-31) and then peel the area (Illus. 4-32).

Remove the burrs from the underside of both blanks. Cut the dorsal fin—and its relief slots—first; then cut the flipper.

Step 9: Saw the Smaller Dolphin

Repeat the procedure described for the larger dolphin in Steps 7 and 8 to cut out the smaller of the two dolphins.

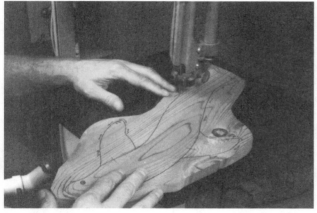

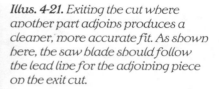

Illus. 4-21. Exiting the cut where another part adjoins produces a cleaner, more accurate fit. As shown here, the saw blade should follow the lead line for the adjoining piece on the exit cut.

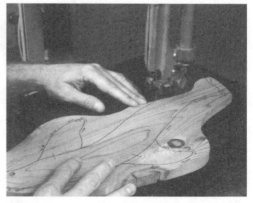

Illus. 4-22. Deburr the bottom of the piece and reposition it before continuing the cut.

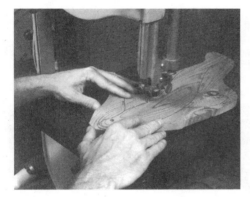

Illus. 4-23. Separate the flipper from the body, keeping the center of the saw blade on the center of the layout line.

Illus. 4-24. Follow the lead line for the nose part to exit the cut.

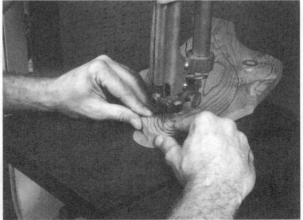

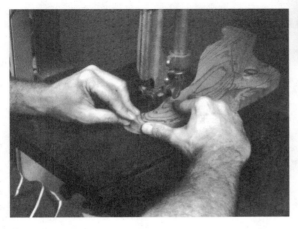

Illus. 4-25. After deburring the piece, replace it on the saw table and begin the cut again. Note that you swing the piece away from the saw column as you cut around the head.

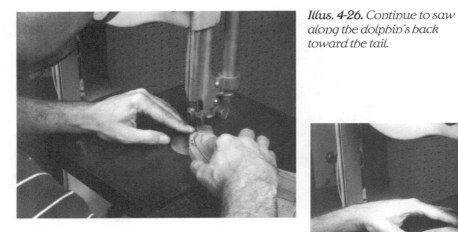

Illus. 4-26. Continue to saw along the dolphin's back toward the tail.

Illus. 4-27. Separate the dorsal fin from the dolphin's body.

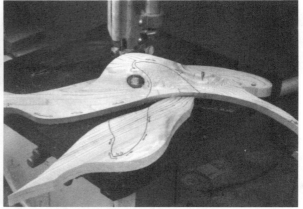

Illus. 4-28. Exit the cut at the end of the tail, sawing straight off the end of the blank.

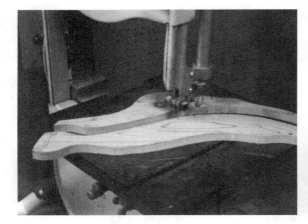

Illus. 4-29. Next saw the dorsal fin and flipper from their blanks. Note the completed body of the larger dolphin underneath the blanks.

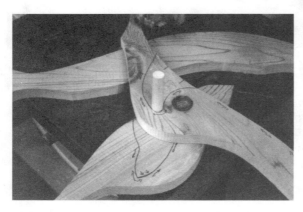

Illus. 4-30. Checking this outside curve with a 1/2" gauge shows that it cannot be cut with a 1/8" wide blade without some preparation.

Illus. 4-31. Cut relief slots around this tight curve before attempting to saw it.

Illus. 4-32. The saw blade peels away the waste wood as it's guided around the curve.

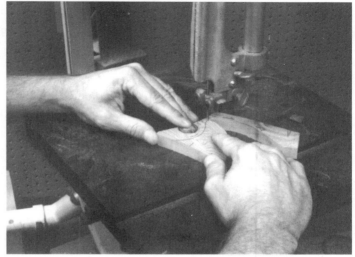

Step 10: Saw the Nose Parts

When you've sawed the body parts for the two dolphins, cut the noses from the remaining dark wood blank. Be sure to check the tight radius with the appropriate plug gauge before beginning to saw. If it is smaller than the plug, cut some relief slots (as for the dorsal fin) and peel the area. (Illustration 4-13 on page 42 shows the peeling process applied to one of the nose parts on this blank.)

Step 11: Saw the White Belly and Mouth Parts

Sand the burrs from the undersides of the white blanks and then cut out the belly and mouth parts. Check the tight radius at the tip of the mouth parts and peel it necessary.

You now have all the parts you'll need to assemble the Dolphins. Chapter 5 explains what to do about any parts that aren't quite right.

Summary of Sawing Sequence

1. Cut laid-out boards into blanks.
2. Sand backs of blanks to remove burrs.
3. Drill parts that call for it.
4. Cross-mark the layout lines of adjoining parts.
5. Check tight curves with a plug gauge.
6. Plan your sawing path.
7. Keep the middle of the saw blade on the middle of the layout line.
8. After every cut, deburr the underside of the piece.

Materials List for the Dolphins

1. Band saw (with 1/8" or 1/4" blade) or scroll saw, for sawing parts
2. Good-quality 6" square, for checking squareness of saw and of parts
3. Sanding block, for removing burrs from blanks
4. Plug gauges: 1/2" diameter plug for 1/8" wide saw blade and 1½" diameter plug for 1/4" wide saw blade.

Chapter 5

Checking the Fit

Checking the Fit

After you have cut out all the parts for your intarsia project, it's time to assemble them and check the fit.

Before doing anything else, however, first use sandpaper to remove any burrs on the undersides of the parts. We generally use fine silicon carbide for this job.

Then, if you numbered the parts when you laid out the project, use the ballpoint pen with which you did the layout to transfer the number on the front of each one to its underside (Illus. 5-1). The reason for this is that the next step—sanding the face of the parts—will remove the numbers. Transferring the numbers preserves them for use in putting the project together.

Now assemble all the parts and see how they fit. You may want to lay the parts out on top of the pattern, using it like a road map.

For the Dolphins: Sand the underside of each part and assemble the Dolphins on the pattern.

Illus. 5-1. Before assembling an intarsia project to check the fit, deburr any rough stuff on the backside of the pieces and, if you numbered your pieces, transfer the numbers to the backs of the parts.

Trimming Parts

Even after years working with intarsia, we still have to trim parts. It's just a step in the process.

It's best to wait until you assemble the project to do any trimming necessary. If you trim a part prematurely, parts you cut later may not fit. The next thing you know, you're adjusting all the parts because you cut a little too much off one of them.

I also prefer to do any trimming before sanding the faces of the parts because the layout lines that remain on the face often indicate which areas need to be trimmed (Illus. 5-2).

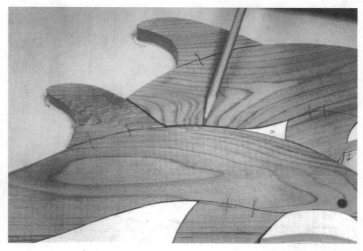

Illus. 5-2. The fit between the two dolphins isn't quite right. Since the layout line is visible, follow it with the saw blade to trim the part to fit.

I trim parts with a saw, rather than sanding their edges to remove extra wood. If you have a way to sand parts while keeping their edges square, go ahead and sand if you find it easier to control the amount of wood you're removing. There are, however, some places a sander just cannot reach.

Determining What/Where to Trim

If the parts are tight, if there is a gap on one end of a part but the other end fits tightly, or if the parts simply don't fit very well but no layout lines remain on them, the best approach is to trim one or more parts in the close-fitting area to make the gaps between all the parts consistent—and therefore, less noticeable.

Carefully mark the area(s) to be trimmed (Illus. 5-3). Follow a variation on the adage "Measure twice, cut once" by checking twice before you trim any part.

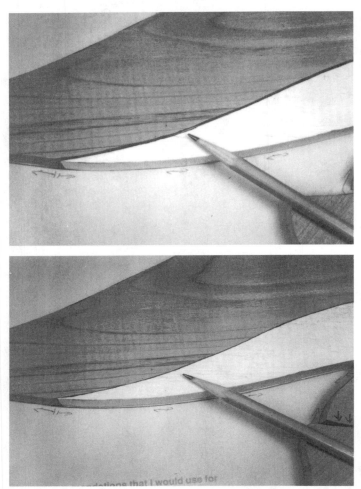

Illus. 5-3. Top: Note the gap (at the lower left in the photograph) between the medium dark part and the light part. The dark part has been marked for trimming, to eliminate the gap. Bottom: Trimming the dark part improves the fit dramatically.

Recutting a Part

Many people—myself included—resist the inclination to recut a part that fits poorly, but sometimes there's no other choice. If it's impossible to trim a part so that it fits properly (if, for example, it's too small), recut the part. Otherwise, you'll see that ill-fitting part every time you look at the finished project. Living with a situation like that is no fun. It's far better to recut the part now and make it right.

For the Dolphins: Trim or recut any Dolphin parts that need adjustment. Then reassemble the project.

Taking a Sneak Preview

If an intarsia composition has a frame, I like to stand the assembled project up and look at it from a distance. (The frame holds the parts together, especially if you lean it a little, even without glue.) For free-form projects like the Dolphins, I use some double-sided tape to attach the parts to a board of some sort so I can stand the project up for a "sneak preview." An alternative is to lay the project out on the floor and then to stand up and step away from it, for a good view.

With the project standing up (Illus. 5-4), take the opportunity to sit down opposite it and catch a second wind. Check how the wood colors and grains work together and plan your next steps. Decide which parts to sand first and what, if any, textures to add (Illus. 5-5). If you decide that any part is too light or too dark, cut a replacement for it before going any further.

For the Dolphins: Tape the Dolphins to a board (or lay them out on the floor) and see how the project looks.

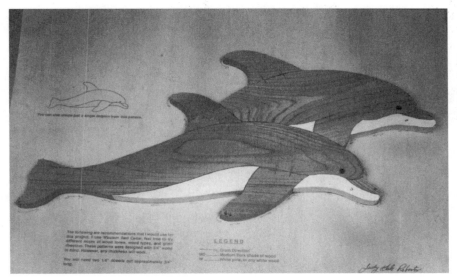

Illus. 5-4. The Dolphins, assembled and with fit problems corrected, are ready for sanding and shaping.

When you are satisfied with the fit and look of everything, you're ready for the next step: sanding and shaping the parts.

Summary of Fit-Checking Sequence

1. Deburr the underside of each part.
2. Number the underside of each part (optional).
3. Assemble the entire project.
4. Check the fit of all parts.
5. Mark parts that need to be trimmed. If the fit is tight at one edge of a part and loose at the other edge, trim the part to make the gaps more consistent.
6. Recut any parts that cannot be trimmed adequately.
7. Reassemble the project. Stand back and look at it to see if the wood colors and grains are working well together.
8. Develop a mental image of what you want the finished project to look like. Plan your approach to sanding and shaping the parts.

Illus. 5-5. This intarsia owl shows how much dimension and texture sanding, shaping, and carving can add to a project.

Materials List for Checking Fit

1. Fine blue or black ballpoint pen, to transfer part numbers to backs of pieces
2. Sandpaper, to remove burrs on backs of parts

Chapter 6

Sanding and Shaping

Sanding and Shaping

Sanding and shaping give an intarsia project its finished quality and let you add dimension to the project if you wish to do so.

Tools for Sanding and Shaping

First let's talk about tools for sanding and shaping your work.

For a number of years, my father and I used only a disc sander and a portable belt sander clamped upside down (with the belt facing up) to a table. Then, while shopping for supplies at our local woodworking-tool dealer, we both spotted a new type of sander on the showroom floor. It was a pneumatic drum sander—and as soon as we had explored it a little, we knew we had to have one.

Disc Sander

A disc sander (Illus. 6-1) makes easy work of rounding pieces, and you can carve or create dips in the wood using the edge of the sander. A disc sander leaves swirls in the wood, but these add interesting textures, giving the wood a rustic look. For a fine finish with a disc sander, you need to follow up with hand-sanding.

If the sandpaper disc is larger than the metal plate of the sander, trim the disc to size. When you use the edge of the disc sander (which you will do quite a bit with intarsia), the excess sandpaper can cause undesirable grooves in the parts.

Belt Sander

With a belt sander (Illus. 6-2), you can sand your wood with the direction of the grain, which produces a smoother finish than sanding against the grain. With the sander mounted upside down, as we do, you can use the little "drum" section at the end of the sander to create dips or carve out areas. Roll your parts over the main (center) section of the belt to round their edges or other areas.

Pneumatic Drum Sander

The drums of a pneumatic drum sander (Illus. 6-3) are not hard, they are positioned at a level that is easy to work at (especially if you are not tall), and you can see the effects of your sanding much more easily than when you're working with a belt sander. (With a belt sander, you must repeatedly flip the wood over to see how things are going.)

Because the drums are flexible (you fill them with air, just like a tire), it's easier to sand soft curves and dips in the wood and you can sand with the wood grain.

My pneumatic drum sander has two sanding drums. I use one drum for heavy sanding ("roughing-in" work) and the other for "clean-up" sanding. I install an 80-grit sleeve on the rough-in drum and start with a 120-grit sleeve on the clean-up drum. Since the Western red cedar that I use is soft,

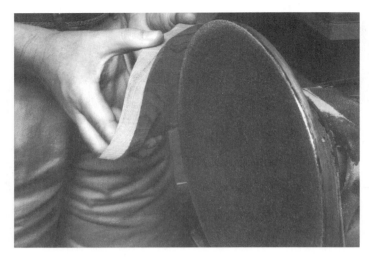

Illus. 6-1. The edge of a disc sander makes a handy carving tool, and its face removes wood quickly.

Illus. 6-2. With a belt sander mounted upside down, you can use the "drum" end sections to create dips and to carve out areas of wood. The center section of the belt sands with the grain and will round edges.

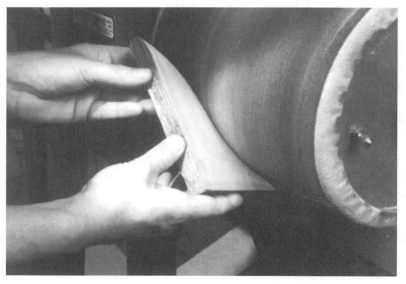

Illus. 6-3. A pneumatic drum sander produces smooth rolling curves. Its soft drums (filled with air just like a tire) make this type of sander easy to work with.

a 120-grit sleeve can easily be too aggressive. To take some of the sharpness out of it, I break in the sleeve so that it "polishes" the wood as I sand. To do this, I install the sleeve on the drum, turn on the sander, and then sand the sleeve with a piece of fine silicon carbide sandpaper. This approach dulls the sleeve more quickly than sanding scrap wood. If you work with hardwoods, you may not want to dull your sleeve. You'll need to experiment.

Although buying a pneumatic drum sander is a big financial commitment to intarsia, the sander is well worth the price if you can afford it.

"Flex" Sander

The "Flex" sander (Illus. 6-4) simulates the action of a pneumatic drum sander. The foamlike cushion that covers the drum of this sander imitates the feel of a pneumatic drum. These sanders work quite well and are much less expensive than pneumatic drums. You purchase the sanding drum(s) separately and then supply your own motor.

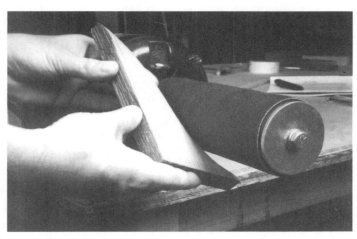

Illus. 6-4. A Flex™ sander behaves much like a pneumatic drum sander, but is much cheaper. Its foamlike cushion simulates the air-filled drum.

Other Tools

Some intarsia buffs use only files, rasps, and sandpaper to finish their projects—and if you enjoy hand-work, you may want to give it a try.

WRC is easy to carve, and I use an X-Acto knife for carving. I also use the knife to smooth or hollow out shapes or areas that are not accessible to a sander.

Some people use a rotary power tool with a small sanding drum attachment. I find that the grinding bit tears up WRC, and cleaning up the mess takes more time than simply carving the piece with a sharp knife. If you are working with hardwood, however, this may not be a problem.

Preparing to Sand and Shape

Before I begin to sand and shape, I collect photographs and other pictures of the subject I'm working on and study them. I keep them out on a table nearby as I sand. These photographs help me form a mental picture of the subject as a living, breathing animal or person or a real-life scene. (A side benefit of this photo research is that the pictures usually inspire me to read about the subject. You'll be amazed at all you learn as you complete one intarsia project after another.)

I also lay out the entire project on a surface near my sanding area so that I can see the whole as I work on each part (Illus. 6-5). I generally lay the wood parts out over the pattern. This lets me work with parts and then return them to the project in just the right location.

Tips for Rough-Sanding and Shaping

Sanding Multiple Parts As One

Most projects contain sections—made up of more than one part—that benefit from being sanded at the same time. Generally, these are entities within the larger project—for example, an animal's body, a tree, or a range of hills. Think of a striped sail on a sailboat. Although the sail is made up of many colors, it is still a flat piece of cloth. You would not want to round the edges of the parts making up the stripes if you were making an intarsia sail.

Look, for example, at the dolphin's body and belly in Illus. 6-6. Although these two parts are cut from different colors of wood, you should sand them as if they were one piece of wood. (They are one piece, in a live dolphin.)

To sand multiple parts as one, first cut a temporary backing for the parts from 1/4" thick scrap plywood (Illus. 6-7). Transfer the outline for the parts to the temporary backing from the pattern (use carbon paper, as when you laid out the pattern on your finish wood earlier), or place the parts on the plywood and trace around them. Use double-sided tape to attach the parts to the backing. Now they are like one piece of wood and can be sanded as one.

*Illus. 6-5. Having the project close at hand as you sand refreshes your memory about how much wood to remove from a part, whether it has an exposed edge, and other aspects of the project as a whole. **Note:** Eye protection and dust mask removed for photography.*

To hold the parts to the temporary backing, I use an inexpensive double-sided white tape sold as carpet tape. The tape, which is 1½" wide, is wider than I prefer, so I cut it lengthwise into thirds (1/2" wide strips) as I

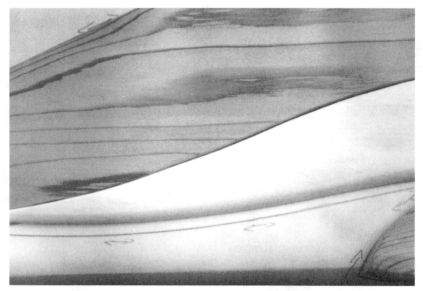

Illus. 6-6. Temporarily assemble parts that make up a "whole" so they can be sanded as one. Although the belly of each dolphin is a different color than the body, these parts are not separate segments in a live dolphin.

Illus. 6-7. To sand multiple parts as one, cut a temporary 1/4" plywood backing piece the same shape as the parts.

use it (Illus. 6-8). Using the least expensive tape I can find and cutting it into narrow strips makes the tape less "aggressive"— easier to remove. I also put the tape in key positions only, using the smallest amount that will do the job. It's a good idea to remove the tape as soon as you can; the longer you leave it in place, the more difficult it is to separate the parts from the backing.

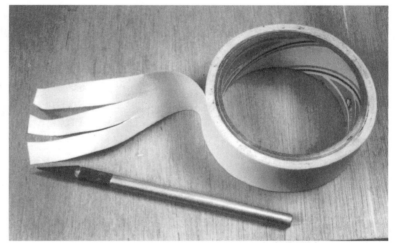

Illus. 6-8. Use double-sided tape to attach intarsia parts to a temporary backing for sanding. Cut the tape into thin (1/2" thick) strips to make it less aggressive.

Pay special attention when attaching small parts to the backing. The sander can grab these small parts, causing problems. To hold a small part in place, put tape along an edge where it adjoins another part, as well as on its underside.

Large gaps caused by missing parts can create "wobble" during sanding. If I think this might be a problem, I'll cut a scrap piece to fill in for the part I don't want to sand with the others.

Sanding parts together saves time. More important, though, it keeps them the same thickness and adds to their unity of effect—rather than making them look like isolated, unrelated segments.

Before you begin to sand a project, check for parts that should be handled as one. Cut temporary backings for each of these areas so that you won't have to stop during sanding to prepare the backings.

Giving Dimension to a Project

Raising Sections. Some intarsia projects benefit from the dimension created when parts are raised above surrounding areas. As mentioned in

Chapter 3, one way to raise a part is by placing a 1/4" plywood shim under it. Raised areas are marked with an "R" (or with "R x 2" for areas to be raised 1/2") on the patterns we offer.

It is best not to raise a part that forms an outside edge, because the viewer will be able to see that the part has been raised when looking at the project from the side. If you must raise a part with an exposed edge, one approach is to laminate a piece of the same wood to the part. When the two layers of wood are the same color, the layering is not too noticeable.

Another way to "raise" an area is to cut the part from thicker (1 ¾") wood.

If a project has raised areas, cut the shims and attach them to the parts at this time, before sanding the project. The Dolphins have no raised areas.

Lowering Sections. If you have cut your intarsia project from nominal 1" boards (3/4" thick), all your parts are the same thickness at this point in the process. To add dimension—and therefore realism—to an intarsia project, you lower some parts to make others appear thicker to the viewer.

Areas of a project that are the farthest from the viewer should be the thinnest. This creates perspective. Parts should be thicker as they "move" closer to the viewer.

Start by first sanding the areas that should be the thinnest. Do a "rough-in" sanding to begin; simply reduce the thickness of the part to your target measurement. (It's frustrating to do the finish shaping on a part only to find you must later modify it to fit an adjoining part.) When you have sanded a part that adjoins another, use a pencil to mark the edge of the (unsanded) adjoining part to show how thick the sanded one is where it touches the unsanded one (Illus. 6-9). When you sand the unsanded part, be sure not to sand below your pencil marks.

After you've established the thicknesses of your parts, then you'll want to taper and/or round the edges of many of them, to give them a realistic look. Use the pencil lines you've made earlier on the edges of the part where others adjoin it to guide you as you round down. You don't want to take off so much wood that an adjoining part will be thicker than the edge you are rounding.

Illus. 6-9. After sanding the dorsal fin of the upper dolphin to a thickness of 1/4", put the fin in place on your layout and mark its depth on the edge of the dolphin's body where the part joins the body.

Sanding dips into pieces or carving out areas also creates dimension within parts.

As you finish rough-sanding a part or a series of parts you are handling as one, return them to the layout. This lets you see how the project is developing, and it also gives you a chance to check that you are keeping the thicknesses of adjoining parts in sync.

Tips for Finish-Sanding and Shaping

Once you've completed all the rough sanding, assemble the entire project, keeping the taped sections still together, and assess your progress. If all the thickness relationships look good and the edges of the parts fit together well, you're ready for the finish (or clean-up) sanding.

On the taped sections, use the sander with a finer grit sandpaper to remove any deep scratches and to sand the exposed edges, removing saw blade marks if any. Before removing these parts from the backing, also hand-sand the areas where the parts adjoin, since the grain directions are the same.

If for one reason or another, things are not as you want them, re-mark areas that need more rough sanding. At this point in some projects, I may tape all the parts to a larger scrap piece of wood so that I can stand the project up to look at it from different angles. I'll use a pencil to shade areas on the face of the wood to be sanded down a little, or to mark other corrections I want to make.

When you've completed the finish sanding, install any dowels (as for the Dolphins), do any wood burning you may desire, or apply stains to areas that might benefit from them. Your project is now ready for finishing.

Step-by-Step Sanding and Shaping Guide for the Dolphins

Step 1: Cut Backings for Unit Sanding

Looking at the Dolphins, you see that you want to sand the body of each dolphin as a unit. The first step is to cut a temporary backing for the four parts that make up the body of each dolphin: the medium dark main body, the nose, and the two white wood belly sections. Use Illus. 6-7 as a guide. (In the photograph, the backings are on top of the project parts so that they are easier to see.) Do not tape the parts to the backings yet.

Step 2: Rough-Sand Dorsal Fin of Upper Dolphin

Look at the Dolphins again. The section farthest from the viewer in this project is the upper dolphin's dorsal fin, so that should be the thinnest part. You'll sand the thinnest parts of the project first, working toward the viewer to the thicker and finally the thickest parts. Since the dorsal fin is a small part, you can safely sand it down to 1/4" thick. Don't worry about contouring at this point; simply reduce the thickness of the part evenly to 1/4". When you've finished sanding the fin, put it back in place on the project layout and use a mechanical pencil to mark its thickness on the edge of the body part where the fin adjoins the body (Illus. 6-9). You'll use this pencil line as a guide (do not sand below it) when you later sand the upper dolphin's back to round and contour its edge.

Step 3: Rough-Sand Body of Upper Dolphin

Moving toward the viewer (and from thinnest to thickest), the next part to sand is the body of the upper dolphin. Take the body parts, turn them upside down, assemble them, and apply double-sided tape to their undersides (Illus. 6-10). Pay attention to the small white belly part, which the sander could grab and separate from the other parts. Put a strip of tape along its edge (Illus. 6-11) before attaching it to the main body of the dolphin. Lay the backing you cut earlier over the parts and press to attach the tape to the backing. Now you're ready to sand the body of the upper dolphin.

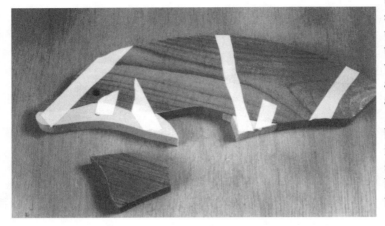

Illus. 6-10. Use strips of double-sided tape to hold the dolphin's body parts together for sanding as a unit.

5/8

Since this dolphin is in the background, prepare to do some heavy sanding with your disc, belt, or other sander. Sanding against the grain removes wood faster than sanding with it. First reduce the thickness of the dolphin's body evenly by about 1/4"— to 1/2" final thickness. Then, taper the "tail" edge of the upper dolphin's body where it adjoins the lower dolphin's dorsal fin to about 3/8" thick (Illus. 6-12). Even though the project is still basically flat, it begins to take on dimension at this point in the rough sanding.

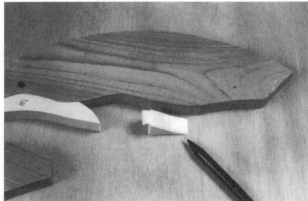

Illus. 6-11. Hold small parts securely for sanding by running a strip of tape along an edge before taping the part to the backing.

Next, round the back of the upper dolphin. (This can be described as "rolling its edge.") Start at the beginning of the back just above the nose and continue all the way to where the back meets the lower dolphin's dorsal fin. In the center of the back, watch for the pencil line you made earlier to show where the upper dolphin's dorsal fin joins its back. Do not sand below that pencil line, or the dolphin's back will be thinner than its dorsal fin where the two join. Illus. 6-13 shows the back after it has been rounded. (Should you accidentally sand too much off the back, mark the dorsal fin so you can sand it down a bit thinner later.)

Illus. 6-12. After sanding the upper dolphin's body to 5/8" thick, taper the edge that touches the lower dolphin's dorsal fin (shown by the pencil at the left) to 3/8" thick.

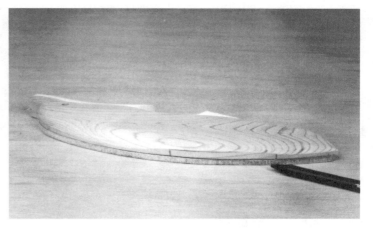

Illus. 6-13. Round the edge of the upper dolphin's back, taking care not to sand below the guideline showing where the dorsal fin joins the back. Take more wood off the areas on either side of the fin than at the juncture of the fin and the body.

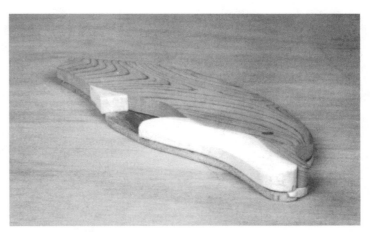

Illus. 6-14. Sand to round the underside of the dolphin's nose (on the white belly section) slightly.

Finally, round the underside (the white wood section) of the dolphin's nose (Illus. 6-14).

Remember, you are just rough-sanding at this point. Don't get carried away trying to make everything exactly perfect.

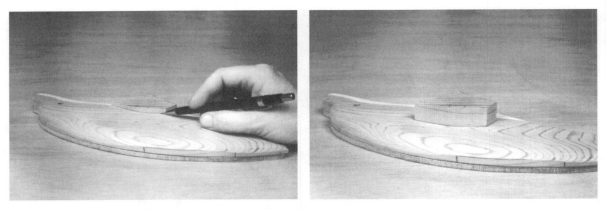

Illus. 6-15. Left: With the flipper in place where it joins the upper dolphin's body, draw a pencil line around its edges to indicate the depth of the body. Right: You'll sand the flipper (now sitting atop the body) to taper its edges down to the lines you drew.

Illus. 6-16. The upper dolphin's flipper, after sanding, gives dimension to the project.

Step 4: Rough-Sand Flipper of Upper Dolphin

With the body of the upper dolphin still taped together (in case you need to sand it further later), put the flipper in place. Mark its edges with a pencil to show the height of the sanded body and the two white belly sections (Illus. 6-15). Then sand the end of the flipper that joins the upper dolphin's body to taper it to match the thickness of the body. Then sand to taper just the edges of the lower section of the flipper to mesh with the white belly sections on either side. As shown in Illus. 6-16, the flipper itself should be thicker than the belly sections; just its edges should be tapered.

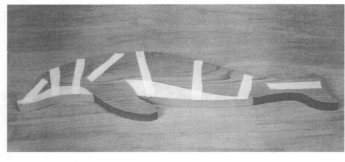

Illus. 6-17. Tape the lower dolphin's body parts for unit sanding. Use the flipper as an aid to position the belly parts during taping.

That finishes the rough-sanding of the upper dolphin. Move on to the lower dolphin. You'll follow the same procedures described in Steps 3 and 4 for rough-sanding the upper dolphin. Only the thicknesses will vary.

Step 5: Prepare Body of Lower Dolphin for Rough-Sanding

Tape the lower dolphin's body parts (everything except the dorsal fin and the flipper) to the sanding backing. Putting the flipper in place while you tape the body parts (as in Illus. 6-17) helps keep the parts in their proper positions. Don't tape the flipper.

Turn the lower dolphin's taped body over on top of the pattern. Put one or more 1/4" shims under the loose dorsal fin of the lower dolphin to raise it to the level of the two dolphin bodies (which are on temporary 1/4" sanding shims). Finally, put the sanded upper dolphin (which is still taped to its sanding

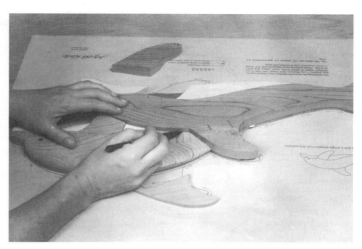

Illus. 6-18. Before sanding the lower dolphin's body, mark the thickness of the upper dolphin on the edges of the lower dolphin's body and dorsal fin. Note the shim under the dorsal fin to raise it 1/4" to the height of the two bodies for marking.

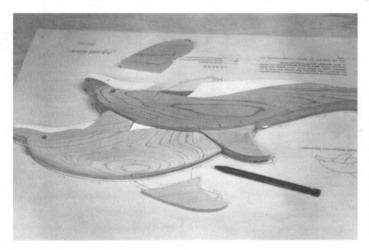

Illus. 6-19. Sand the lower dolphin's dorsal fin to a "stair-step" thickness between that of the upper dolphin's body and the lower dolphin's body. Mark its thickness on the edge of the lower dolphin's back before sanding the body of the lower dolphin.

backing) in place on the pattern. As in Illus. 6-18, use a pencil to mark the edges of the lower dolphin's body and dorsal fin where they join the upper dolphin.

Step 6: Rough-Sand Dorsal Fin of Lower Dolphin

Since the dorsal fin of the lower dolphin is the farthest part of this dolphin from the viewer, sand it to 1/2" thick (an intermediate step between the thickness of the upper dolphin's body and the thickness you will make the lower dolphin's body). Watch for the pencil line on its edge showing the thickness of the upper dolphin; don't sand the fin thinner than that line.

When the fin is sanded to a 1/2" thickness (Illus. 6-19), put it back on the layout and mark its thickness on the edge of the lower dolphin's back. Now you're ready to sand the body of the lower dolphin.

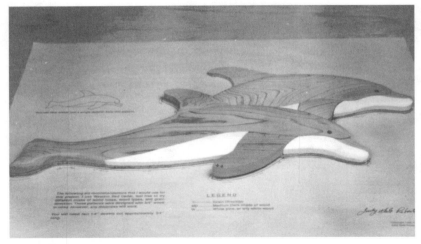

Step 7: Rough-Sand Body of Lower Dolphin

Sand the taped body parts of the lower dolphin, tapering the back slightly toward the nose and down toward the tail.

Next round all the exposed edges, being careful not to sand below any pencil lines marking areas where parts join (Illus. 6-20).

I like to sand some dips in this dolphin's tail (Illus.

Illus. 6-20. The Dolphins, with all rough sanding except the lower flipper completed. Note how much thicker the flipper is before sanding than the rest of the body.

6-21). You can carve the dips or make them with the edge of a disc sander or the drum area of a belt sander. (I use my pneumatic drum sander.) Since the grain runs lengthwise on the tail, I have to sand across it to make the dips. I hand-sand the area later, to smooth it out.

Step 8: Rough-Sand Flipper of Lower Dolphin

When you're satisfied with the roughed-in shape of the lower dolphin, put it on the pattern, put the flipper in place, and mark the edges of the flipper where they contact the body and belly parts of the dolphin. Sand the upper portion of the flipper to taper it to the same thickness as the lower dolphin's body. I also sand a slight dip on the back side of the flipper, in the area where it curves. Remember that this flipper is the closest part of the project to the viewer. Keep it thicker than all the other parts.

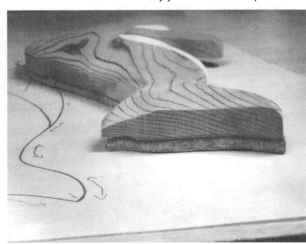

Illus. 6-21. Sanding dips into the dolphin's tail adds realism to the project.

Step 9: Assemble Dolphins and Finish-Sand Project

Now assemble the entire project, keeping the taped units together, and see how things look. If you find problems, mark those parts for resanding and correct whatever you feel needs work before cleaning up the parts.

If everything looks good, still keeping the parts taped to their backings, finish-sand deep scratches from the faces of all parts, finish-sand all exposed edges, and hand-sand the areas where the parts join. Then remove all the parts from their backings.

Step 10: Sand and Shape Noses of Dolphins

Round the upper (exposed) edge of each dolphin's dark wood nose. Then put the nose in position and mark the edge of the head to show where the nose meets it (Illus 6-22 top). Next, taper the edge of the head to match the nose (Illus. 6-22 bottom).

I also hand-sand to round the edges where the dark nose and the white section meet. This seems to accentuate the "smile" that we see when we look at a dolphin.

Step 11: Make Eyes for the Dolphins

I use a wood burner to burn around the circumference of the holes drilled earlier for the eyes, to remove burrs and rough edges. I also use the burner to give "corners" to the eyes (Illus. 6-23). If you don't have access to a wood burner, carving can create the same effect.

The Dolphins call for 1/4" dowel for making the eyes. I first round each end of the uncut dowel. (Keeping it its full length makes it easier to work with). Since I want the dolphin's eyes to be dark, I use the flat tip (intended for shading) of my wood burner to darken the rounded ends. (Alternatives are to stain the dowel ends or to use dark walnut dowels.) Then I carefully sand one edge of the rounded dowel (eye), making it light and giving the eye direction (Illus. 6-24).

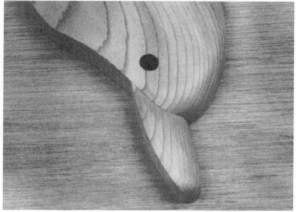

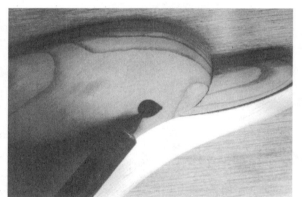

Illus. 6-23. Using a wood burner, burn the inside circumference of the hole drilled for the eye. Then use the burner to make corners on the eye.

Illus. 6-22. Top: After sanding each dolphin's nose to taper it toward the exposed edge, mark the depth of the nose on the edge of the head. Bottom: Then taper the head toward the nose, imitating the bulblike look of a bottle-nose dolphin's head.

Illus. 6-24. After rounding and then burning the end of a 1/4" dowel, sand one edge to give the eye direction.

Insert the dowel from the back of the head so that the rounded section of the dowel is slightly above the wood surface; mark the length for cutting. Repeat for the other eye using the opposite end of the dowel.

Illus. 6-25. These two views of the Dolphins show how the parts should be sanded and shaped to give the project dimension. Areas farther from the viewer are thinner; those closer are thicker. Exposed edges are rounded, and areas where parts join are hand-sanded for smoothness.

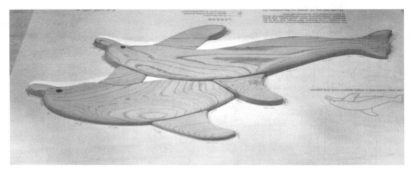

Put the dowel eye in place (I like to rotate the eye so that it appears as if the dolphin is looking back at the viewer), check its length, glue it in place, and then cover the area on the back of the part where the dowel is glued with some masking tape so that you can turn the part over without worrying about oozing glue. Repeat for the other eye. Remove the tape when the eye is dry.

Illus. 6-25 shows two views of the Dolphins with all sanding and shaping completed. They are ready to finish.

Summary of Sanding and Shaping Sequence

1. Familiarize yourself with the subject matter of the project. (Study photographs and/or books.)

2. Plan your approach:

    a. Identify parts that should be sanded together.

    b. Plan ways to add dimension to the project—by raising or lowering one or more parts.

    c. Decide which parts should be the thinnest (those farthest from the viewer) and which should be the thickest (those closest to the viewer). Sand the thinnest parts first. Work your way to the thickest parts.

3. Make temporary sanding backings from 1/4" thick scrap plywood

for parts to be sanded as one. Transfer the outline of the parts to the plywood from the pattern, or trace around the parts.

4. Use double-sided tape to attach parts to the temporary backings.

5. Rough-sand to establish all thicknesses and shapings, using a pencil to mark the edges of adjoining parts for thickness as you sand.

6. After everything is rough-sanded to your satisfaction but before removing any parts from their backings, do some clean-up sanding with your sander and/or by hand.

7. Remove all parts from their temporary sanding backings.

Summary of Sanding and Shaping Sequence for the Dolphins

1. Sand the upper dolphin first. Use a temporary backing for all the body parts except the dorsal fin and the flipper.

2. Sand the lower dolphin next. Use a temporary backing for all the body parts except the dorsal fin and the flipper.

3. Complete the eyes: Burn (or carve) corners. Round and then burn (or stain) the dowel tips. Insert dowel tips in predrilled holes, measure and trim, and glue in place.

Materials List for Dolphins

1. Sander (pneumatic drum, belt, disc) or rasps

2. Scrap plywood 1/4" thick, for making temporary sanding backings

3. Double-sided tape, for attaching parts to temporary backings

4. Mechanical pencil, for transferring outlines to backings and for marking edges for thickness

5. One 1/4" dowel, for the eyes of the dolphins

6. Wood burner or sharp carving knife, to complete the dolphins' eyes

Intarsia Projects:
a Gallery of Finished Examples

Hidden Forest — a forest scene with six different animals, measures 32" x 38" and contains 556 different pieces. It has won numerous prizes, including First Place for Applied Relief (Intarsia), in international competition at the 1988 Canadian National Exhibition.

New Shoes — a 24" x 37" panel of a young boy splashing water on his new shoes, contains 187 different pieces of wood. It took First Place in Applied Relief (Intarsia) at the 1989 Canadian National Competition.

Cow. This endearing piece is an intermediate level project. 115 pieces, 18" x 17"

❖ **Easy to Make Inlay Wood Projects—Intarsia** ❖

Hobo Clown. Intermediate level. 22" x 16"—73 pieces.

Big Foot Clown. Intermediate level. 22" x 16"—66 pieces.

❖ Easy to Make Inlay Wood Projects–Intarsia ❖

Teddy Bears. 30 pieces per bear. 10.5" x 7.5" The unique stitching effect was created with a wood burning tool. Good beginners' pieces.

The frame around this portrait of an **Indian Chief** really adds to this piece. A project for the Intermediate/expert level. 22" x 22" 183 pieces.

❖ Easy to Make Inlay Wood Projects—Intarsia ❖

This **tiger** and the **elephant** below are from Judy's Endangered Wildlife series. Each is 19" x 19" and is an intermediate level project. Tiger contains 92 pieces, the elephant 77 pieces.

❖ **Easy to Make Inlay Wood Projects—Intarsia** ❖

Eagle Landing. 23" x 34" — 126 pieces. This beautiful piece is of intermediate/expert difficulty.

Buffalo-31" x 18.75" contains 66 pieces. Intermediate/expert level.

❖ Easy to Make Inlay Wood Projects—Intarsia ❖

These curious, energetic raccoons are very popular creations and illustrate how a well-designed project can really have "personality".

Curious Coon is an intermediate level project 15" x 20.5" with 55 pieces **Out on a Limb** is an intermediate/expert project — 34" x 14" with 86 pieces.

❖ **Easy to Make Inlay Wood Projects—Intarsia** ❖

Still Pottery. 12.5" x 22.25", 84 pieces. Beginner to intermediate level.

Rocky Top. Beginner/intermediate level. 15" x 19"-72 pieces.

❖ Easy to Make Inlay Wood Projects—Intarsia ❖

Eagle. 15" x 37"-92 pieces. Intermediate/expert level.

Chapter 7

Hand-Sanding and Finishing

Hand-Sanding and Finishing

When you're satisfied with the shaping of your project, you're ready to hand-sand all the parts and then to apply the finish to them.

Hand-Sanding

The object of hand-sanding is to remove any sharp scratches left by the sander and to soften the edges of each part. We call this process detailing. It adds the special touch that only hand-work can produce.

Using the Dolphins as an example, Illus. 7-1 shows the results of detailing. Note how much smoother and more graceful the juncture between the dark and light body parts appears after the edges of the parts have been hand-sanded.

When hand-sanding, it helps to give your attention completely to each individual part. For now, forget about the project as a whole.

For hand-sanding, use a high-quality 180-, 220-, or 240-grit sandpaper. You may wish to begin with a 180 grit sandpaper and move to a 220 grit on project areas that require heavy sanding. I prefer a silicon carbide paper with a stearate coating. This paper is white or light gray in color, not black. Many companies make silicon carbide papers, but not all of these papers are "created equal." Although it can be difficult to find, I prefer the nonloading silicon carbide paper—called Sun Gold—made by Sun Abrasives Co. Sun Gold is an extremely sharp paper with excellent cutting ability, even in the fine grits. (See the Buyer's Guide for a catalog source for the Sun paper.)

Sun Gold is sold in 9" x 11" sheets. I divide each large sheet into nine smaller sheets and then fold each small sheet in half to produce a piece with grit on both outside surfaces (Illus. 7-2). To sand with these smaller sheets, I place the unfolded edge between my index and middle fingers so that my thumb is on the fold (Illus. 7-3). I use my thumb to apply cutting pressure during sanding. With my thumb, it's easy to control the amount of pressure (increasing or decreasing it as necessary).

Before beginning to hand-sand the project, wash your hands thoroughly to remove any oils or dirt and do not eat or snack while you are finish-sanding. Freshly sanded wood acts like a sponge, soaking up any oils on your fingers. When you apply the first coat of finish, these oils show up as light or dark spots on your parts.

Edge Sanding

Working with one part at a time, lightly sand over each edge to round it. You may want to round some edges more than others; it depends on the effect you're trying to achieve. If you are new to intarsia, at first just soften all the edges equally. As you gain more experience, you can experiment with different effects during hand-sanding.

Illus. 7-1. Top: In this example from the Dolphins, the edges of the dark and light body parts show roughness before hand-sanding. Bottom: Note the improvement in the appearance of the two pieces after hand-sanding. The edges of the parts are slightly rounded and much smoother, and the grain on the surface of the white belly section has a finer look.

Face Sanding

When you have finished all the edge work, you may wish to lightly sand the face of each part to remove any scratches left by the power sander. Face-sanding is a matter of individual taste. Some people like a rougher, more rustic finish; others prefer the smooth, fine surface produced by hand-sanding. If you are just getting started with intarsia, extensive face-sanding isn't necessary. Simply brush the face of each part lightly with sandpaper to remove any "ticks."

Dusting the Parts

When you've finished the detail work, remove all the sawdust from the parts. I use compressed air to blow off the dust, being careful to clean the back and all the edges of the parts as well as their faces. If you don't have a compressor, use a soft-bristle brush to dust each part thoroughly.

Also, whether you're finishing furniture or an intarsia project, be sure your work area is clean and completely free from dust.

Choosing a Finishing Method

Through trial and error, we've developed a finishing method that works very well for us. We finish each individual intarsia part separately, before gluing the project together.

In the past we first glued the project and then spray-finished the entire piece at one time. That approach saved time, but we felt it reduced the quality of the finished project. The technique we use now takes more time, but it produces a result that is far superior in quality to the spray finish—and that's just what we want.

Illus. 7-2. Cut a large sheet of fine-grit silicon carbide sandpaper into manageable sizes for hand-sanding. Fold the smaller pieces in half to create a piece with grit on both outside surfaces.

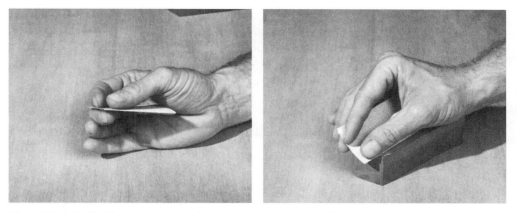

Illus. 7-3. Left: Hold the folded sandpaper between your index and middle fingers, with your thumb over the fold. Right: Apply cutting pressure with your thumb.

There are two reasons why finishing individual parts produces a higher quality result. For one thing, if glue comes in contact with the face of an unfinished part, it leaves a light spot even if it is wiped off immediately. The only way to remove the spot is to resand the area thoroughly (and deeply) before applying the finish. That can be quite a problem if you drip glue on a cluster of parts or can't remember exactly where you dripped the glue after you wipe it up.

Second, our intarsia projects are rarely flat; most of the parts have different thicknesses. Our projects also contain many different parts, few of which have the grain running in the same direction. These characteristics make it almost impossible to apply a quality finish if the project is glued together before finishing. It is very difficult to sand each part with the grain between finish coats without sanding the parts next to it; it is also almost impossible to sand tiny points of wood adjoining other parts.

These days we use a wiping gel finish. It's very easy to apply and has a smooth, professional look, even though we put it on with a "brush." Almost anyone—experienced or inexperienced—can produce a professional result with a wiping gel. This is not the case with a spray finish, where technique can make or break the final appearance.

Applying a Wiping Gel Finish

To apply a wiping gel finish, you simply brush the material on, wait no longer than a couple of minutes, and then wipe the gel off with a paper towel or rag. When the first coat has dried, you apply a second, and then a third. A wiping gel produces a glossy finish.

Collect all the supplies you'll need before you begin to apply the finish. For the wiping gel finish, you'll need a can of gel varnish, a disposable 1" wide foam brush, and a supply of good-quality paper towels or rags (Illus. 7-4). When you open the gel varnish, you'll find it's thick and creamy, the consistency of pudding. Be sure to use a new foam brush. (No matter how well you've cleaned it, a used brush could hold old residue that

Illus. 7-4. For a professional finish on intarsia projects, use a foam brush to apply three coats of a clear wiping gel like the one shown here. Wipe the gel off with folded paper towels.

might dissolve in the gel and produce an unwanted color in your finish.) I prefer paper towels to rags. Rags dry hard, making them suitable for one-time use only, and they have a tendency to leave lint on the work. Before beginning to apply the finish, tear 10 to 15 individual paper towels off the roll and fold them into quarters (Illus. 7-5). Check the finishing area for dust.

First Coat

Load the new brush well with the gel, and apply it to the first part (Illus. 7-6). It makes no difference which part you start with. After you have applied finish to a few parts, the brush becomes saturated with the gel and requires addition of only a little more gel for each new part. Apply the finish to the face of the part first, then to the sawed edges. For the first coat, lay the finish on thick. (You can apply the second and third coats more sparingly.) This is especially true for WRC, which really soaks up the varnish, and less so for a hardwood. If the gel starts to dry while you are still applying it, go over the dry spot again with fresh gel.

Illus. 7-5. Wiping gel tacks up quickly after application, and must be wiped off within a few minutes. Before starting the first coat, prepare a supply of paper towels by separating them from the roll and folding them into quarters. Turn the towels often and replace them with clean ones as they become wet with gel.

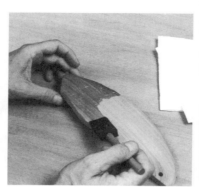

Illus. 7-6. Using a heavily loaded brush for the first coat, cover the raw wood thickly with gel, working with the grain. Apply the gel in the direction of the grain for best results. Note how the finish darkens the wood a shade, returning it close to its color when wet.

Applying the finish to the wood turns it one shade darker, returning the wood almost to the color it was when it was wet. The finish also gives our WRC a rich appearance; it no longer looks like an inexpensive softwood.

When the face and edges of the first part are thoroughly coated, place it to the side and apply finish to the next part. Should your finger contact the face of a part after you have applied the finish to it, simply dab a little more finish on the fingerprint after you lay the part down.

If you're working by yourself, coat only three or four parts (Illus. 7-7) before beginning to wipe the finish off. Don't let more than a few minutes go by between applying and removing the gel. Wipe both the face and the edges until the part, especially the face, looks dry. Don't be stingy with the paper towels. Fold wet towel sections into the center and change to clean, dry towels often. Although wiping the finish off so thoroughly may seem to defeat the purpose, the finish builds up as you apply the second and third coats.

Coat and wipe the parts in small groups, moving on to a second and then a third set of parts when you finish coating and wiping the first set.

If you wait too long before wiping off the gel, it will start to tack up. Your towel or rag will stick to the part, rather than glide over it. If this happens, don't panic. Simply apply another coat of gel over the first one. Wait a minute or so for the fresh gel to soften the tacky first coat. Then wipe everything off.

Illus. 7-7. Coat only three or four parts at a time. Wipe those off and then coat the next group. Note the thickness of this first-coat gel application.

Note for corners and holes: It can be difficult to wipe gel out of inside corners or holes in parts. To remove gel from a tight area, I use a blast of compressed air. First wipe the face and edges of the part, then direct the air on the area that needs it. The air pressure solidifies the gel and makes it run out of the tight area. Use a pressure of about 30 psi. (Too much pressure can blow the part out of your hand, possibly breaking it.) After applying the air, check to see if any gel has blown out onto the face of the part; if it has, rewipe that area immediately because the gel will dry very fast after the air has contacted it.

As you coat and wipe each set of parts, spread them out on a clean surface to dry. You may want to lay them out as they will be in the finished project so you can see how they look. Be sure to leave air space between the parts.

When you've applied the first coat to all the parts, replace the lid on the can of gel varnish and close it tightly (Illus. 7-8). Also immediately wrap the foam brush with aluminum foil or plastic wrap; wrapping it keeps it usable for several days.

Wait 15 minutes. Then pick up a part and run your fingers over the face. The face should feel dry; only the sawed edges may feel a little tacky. At this point you no longer need to worry about dust getting on the parts. As an experiment, you could sprinkle some sawdust on a part; it won't stick. This should help you understand why we have switched to the wiping gel finishing method.

Illus. 7-8. As you finish wiping the parts, set them aside to dry, laying them out as in the finished project if you wish to. Be sure to leave space around all parts to encourage even drying. Tightly close the gel container; wrap the brush in plastic wrap or aluminum foil to keep it soft for the next coat.

*Illus. 7-9. When apply-
ing the second and
third coats of wiping
gel, recoat the edges of
the parts only if they—
like the lower dolphin's
flipper—form an out-
side edge on a free-
form project.*

Second Coat

Now let the project dry for four to six hours. Do not apply the second coat any sooner.

The second coat (and the third) goes much more quickly because in most cases you need to apply the gel only to the face of the parts, not to their edges. The exception is if a part's edge forms the outer edge of a free-form project (Illus. 7-9). Recoat those outer edges also.

Give the second coat time to dry thoroughly. This will take four to six hours like the first coat.

Third Coat: A Decision

Now you must decide what degree of gloss you want your finish to have. This is a matter of personal taste.

Gloss Finish. The wiping gel produces a shiny (gloss) finish. If you prefer that type of finish, go over each part of your intarsia project with #00 steel wool before applying the third coat of wiping gel. Be sure to blow or brush off the parts to remove any steel wool particles when you've finished.

Apply the third coat of wiping gel exactly as you did the second. Allow it to dry (overnight is best) and then you're ready to glue the project together.

Matte Finish. We prefer a matte finish on our intarsia projects. To produce that type of finish, we spray the project with a matte finish after gluing it together. The spray dulls the gloss of the wiping gel finish to our liking.

If you want the type of matte finish we prefer, apply the third coat of wiping gel directly over the second one after it has dried. (Do not rub the parts with steel wool between the two coats.) Let the third coat dry thoroughly—overnight is best. Then use #00 steel wood to lightly go over each part, to dull the glossy finish of the gel to help the matte spray adhere to the project. (You'll find instructions for applying the matte spray after gluing in Chapter 10.)

When the third coat of wiping gel has dried, take a good look at the finish. You'll see that it looks very professional: no heavy build-up and no drips, runs, or brush marks. This is why we use a wiping gel finish exclusively on our projects.

Summary of Hand-Sanding and Finishing Sequence

1. Prepare silicon carbide sandpaper.
2. Lightly sand all sharp edges to smooth them.
3. Clean all parts. Use blasts of compressed air or a brush.
4. Handling a few parts at a time, brush on the first coat of wiping gel, wait a few minutes, and then wipe thoroughly.
5. Wait the recommended drying time. Apply the second, and then the third, coat of wiping gel, allowing the coats to dry thoroughly between applications.

Option: For a gloss finish, rub the parts gently with #00 steel wool between the second and third coats. For a matte finish, use the #00 steel wool after the third coat has dried; spray the project after assembly with a matte finish.

Materials List for Dolphins

1. Fine-grit (180- to 240-grit) silicon carbide sandpaper
2. Air compressor or soft brush, for removing sawdust from parts
3. Clear wiping gel varnish
4. Disposable 1" foam brush, for applying the varnish
5. Good-quality paper towels or rags, for wiping off the gel
6. #00 steel wool, for roughing up finish surface before applying final finish coat

Chapter 8

Final Layout and Backing

Final Layout and Backing

We use 1/4" thick lauan plywood as a backing for our intarsia projects. The plies are generally consistent, with few voids. If you prefer, you can use 1/8" thick lauan. Some folks use Masonite, but we've found it has a tendency to warp.

For free-form intarsia projects, it's best to cut the backing after you have sanded, shaped, and finished all the parts. As you sand individual parts to clean up saw marks on their edges—especially parts on the outer edges of a project—you change their size slightly. Using the final size and shape of parts as a guide to cut the backing gives you the freedom to move parts a little this way or that or to tighten them up a bit when you do the final layout. If you cut the backing earlier, directly from the pattern, you may have to adjust the parts to fit the backing or trim the backing to fit the parts—neither of which is desirable.

Laying Out the Project and Transferring the Outline to the Backing

The most accurate way to transfer the outline of a project to the backing wood is to trace around the edge of the laid-out project with a mechanical pencil. First cover the backing with paper, to keep the pencil from catching in the wood grains as you draw the outline and to make it easier to see the pencil line.

Attaching the Paper

Use a repositionable spray adhesive (the kind marked "for permanent or temporary bonds") to attach the paper to the backing wood. Some brands of spray adhesive are more aggressive than others. Before applying the paper to your backing wood, experiment with some scrap wood. Determine how much adhesive to apply to the paper, how long to let the adhesive dry before placing the paper on the wood, and how easy it will be to remove the paper from the backing after you've cut out the backing piece.

When you've completed the tests, cut a piece of white paper large enough for the project. (You can buy plain white paper in rolls, in various widths, for this purpose.) Spray the back of the paper with the adhesive, let the adhesive dry a few minutes, and then place the paper carefully on the plywood backing sheet (Illus. 8-1).

Next, spray a very light coat of adhesive on the face of the paper and let it dry briefly. This tacky surface keeps the intarsia parts from sliding around on the slick surface of the paper while you trace the project outline. (Another intarsia enthusiast wrote us to share that idea. Although some folks think that all these steps make an intarsia project more time-

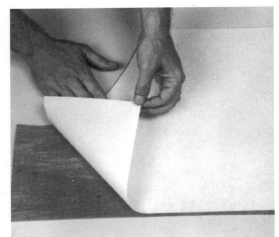

Illus. 8-1. Apply spray adhesive to a large sheet of white paper, let the adhesive tack up, and smooth the paper over the plywood backing material.

consuming than it need be, it's actually the other way around. Improving accuracy actually saves time and reduces frustrations caused by fit problems.)

Laying Out the Project

Now lay out all the parts of the intarsia project on the paper, as if you were ready to glue them down. Look the project over carefully as you put it together, checking for gaps and adjusting the spacing around parts.

A word about spacing: To accentuate a line, leave a gap just shy of 1/16" between two parts. On the Dolphins, you might, for example, want to leave a gap between the dark nose section and the white mouth, to accentuate the smile (Illus. 8-2). If the space is tight on one side of a part but loose on the other side, adjust the part to even up the space all the way around it. You don't want to hide the fact that your intarsia project is made up of individual pieces of wood.

Tracing the Outline

Then use a mechanical pencil to carefully draw completely around the project. Check the outline for completeness before removing any of the parts. Then carefully set the parts aside (Illus. 8-3) and get ready to cut the backing piece.

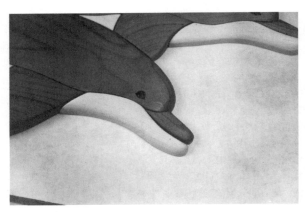

Illus. 8-2. Intentional gaps between parts intensify the separation between them. The gap between the dolphin's dark nose part and its white mouth part points up the smile.

Cutting, Staining, and Sealing the Backing

Depending on the size of your project, you can cut the backing with a saber saw, a band saw, or even a scroll saw. Cut just to the inside of the pencil outline, so that the backing will be a hair smaller than the project. This gives you some leeway when it's time to glue the parts to the backing.

After the backing is cut out, remove the paper and then sand off any burr produced by the saw blade. We use a shoe dye or a shoe edge dye to stain the edges of the backing a dark brown (Illus. 8-4). Shoe dye is alcohol based and dries quickly. (At this stage of the project, you don't want to wait for things to dry.) Staining the edges dark minimizes the degree to which they detract from the intarsia piece itself.

We have had bad experiences applying stain to the backside of the backing; it causes the backing to warp or twist. However, some people have good results using spray paint to darken the edges and the back of the backing. Since the spray paint dries quickly, it does not seem to cause warping.

Do not stain or seal the face of the backing. Since you glue the parts to it, the face should be as porous as possible.

When the stain on the edges of the backing is dry, I sand the backside of the backing with an orbital sander, to remove any stain that dripped or ran in the grain and to make the backside of the project look as attractive as possible.

I then coat the backside and the edges of the backing with a clear spray sealer. When using spray paints and sealers, be sure to follow all the safety precautions on the can. We need to protect all the brain cells we are born with.

When the backing is ready, it's time to glue the parts to it.

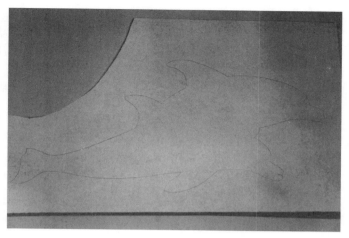

Illus. 8-3. Outlining the project on paper produces a smooth and accurate line for cutting the backing to the correct shape.

Illus. 8-4. Staining the edges of the backing dark brown makes them less distracting to the viewer.

Summary of Final Layout and Backing Sequence

1. Affix white paper to the plywood backing material with repositionable spray adhesive.

2. Spray the face of the paper with a light coat of adhesive.

3. Lay out all the project parts, checking them for fit and adjusting the space around them as needed.

4. Trace the outline of the project onto the white paper with a mechanical pencil.

5. Use a saw to cut slightly inside the pencil outline, making the backing piece slightly smaller than the project.

6. Dye, stain, or spray-paint the edges of the backing a dark brown.

7. Sand the backside of the backing to remove excess stain and then seal it with a clear spray sealer.

Materials List for Dolphins

1. Lauan plywood (1/4" or 1/8" thick), for backing the project

2. White paper (at least 23" x 11") on which to trace the project outline

3. Spray can of repositionable adhesive, to affix the paper to the backing board

4. Saw (band, scroll, or saber), to cut the backing

5. Dark brown dye, stain, or spray paint, to color the edges of the backing

6. Sandpaper, to smooth the underside of the backing

7. Can of clear spray sealer, to seal the edges and back of the backing

Chapter 9

Gluing

Gluing

With the backing cut, it's time to glue the project to it. At this point, it feels like we're walking on eggshells. We've made it this far, with no major problems. We just hope everything else goes as well.

Assembling the Project on the Backing

Assemble the finished parts on the backing. Check the spacing between them. Remember, try to keep the spacing around parts even. If the space is tight on one side of a part and loose on the other, even out the difference. If you can't fix a gap by repositioning the parts, use a dark brown felt-tipped pen to darken the backing where the gap occurs (Illus. 9-1). The light backing telegraphs the gap, but darkening the space makes it almost disappear.

Selecting an Adhesive

We use both hotmelt adhesive and yellow wood glue to attach an intarsia project to its backing (Illus. 9-2).

Hotmelt adhesive is used in many types of craft projects; it's great for quick bonds. You can purchase the adhesive (which is sold in sticks) and an application gun at most craft supply and discount stores. For intarsia, hotmelt adhesive works like a clamp, securing the part until the wood glue has time to set up. You need only a few dots of hotmelt adhesive to do the job. Its drawbacks? It's very stringy, it sets up very quickly, and the bond it creates can pop loose, especially if subjected to intense heat. We feel its benefits outweigh its drawbacks, however, for assembling intarsia projects.

Illus. 9-1. Darkening the backing with a brown marker before gluing the parts to it makes gaps between parts less obvious.

If you've never worked with hotmelt adhesive, experiment before starting to glue your intarsia project. Practice using the glue gun and see how fast the adhesive sets up. This determines how much time you have to put a part in place after you've applied the adhesive to it. If you do not put the part down fast enough, the hotmelt will set up and keep the part from sitting flush on the backing.

Gluing Sequence

I use the hotmelt adhesive/wood glue combination only to attach "anchor" parts—parts on the outside edges of the project that determine the position of all the other parts. To attach the remainder of the parts, I use only wood glue.

Illus. 9-2. Yellow wood glue (upper left) is the basic adhesive for attaching intarsia parts to the backing. For the best results—especially on exterior anchor parts—use it in conjunction with hot-melt adhesive (sticks and application gun shown at upper right).

Free-form Projects

Free-form projects, like the Dolphins, have no frame to hold the parts in place as you glue them. When gluing a free-form project, glue the outside parts first, working your way around the project. Then glue the interior parts in place.

Framed Projects

When gluing a framed project, spacing is critical. Everything must fit within the confines of the frame. When my father and I first put intarsia projects in frames, the interior parts seemed to "grow"—they were always larger than the pattern. Today, we rarely need to trim parts to make them fit the frame; our projects seem to shrink.

When working with a framed piece, the object is to make sure that any gap between the parts and the frame is consistent all the way around (Illus. 9-3). A gap that is consistent visually disappears. If the gap is inconsistent when you lay out the project, determine what the largest gap is—for example, 1/8" or 1/4"—and then trim the edges of all outside parts so they are equally short of the frame.

My father referred to the "gap" between project and frame as a reveal, a term that certainly sounds much better than gap. He treated the reveal as an intentional feature.

Intarsia is an art form that viewers like to examine very closely. They want to see how it is put together. We've found that when a piece catches someone's attention, he or she tends to walk right up to it and examine it from about 2" away. When people look at intarsia at such close range, they are quick to point out gaps. They are less likely to be concerned about them when all the spaces are even.

During gluing, we use homemade "spacers" to keep the reveal between the frame and the project even on all four sides. We make our spacers from old cardboard notebook backs, cutting them in strips about 1" x 11" (or whatever the length of the cardboard is). Depending on the reveal we want, we insert one, two, or even three strips (thicknesses) along the edge of the frame. I tape these strips to the frame, to keep them from falling over when I remove a wood part to apply adhesive to it (Illus. 9-4).

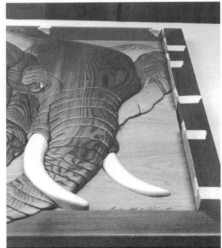

Illus. 9-3. Homemade cardboard spacers keep the gap between project and frame consistent on all four sides during gluing. Tape the spacers to the frame to hold them in place.

As with a free-form project, I use a combination of hotmelt adhesive and wood glue to affix all edge parts in a framed piece to the backing. The hotmelt "clamps" the parts securely against the edge I've established to ensure an even reveal around the project when the wood glue dries.

When you have glued down all the edge parts in a framed project, check the spacing between all the remaining parts. If there are any gaps, spread out all the remaining parts a little to take up the difference. Then use wood glue alone to attach the interior parts.

Gluing Techniques

To glue intarsia, apply the adhesive to the part, not to the backing. For anchor parts, first apply a few dots of wood glue to the back; then, a few dots of the hotmelt adhesive. Leave space between the two adhesives because the wood glue will cool the hotmelt if it touches it, reducing the hotmelt's bonding strength. Don't flood the back of the part with wood glue. A few dots go a long way. Because WRC absorbs moisture from the wood glue, a heavy application can cause parts to warp.

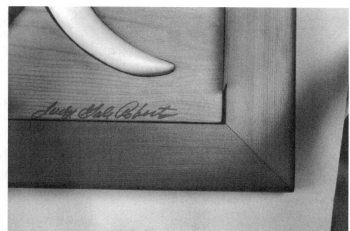

Illus. 9-4. In this example, the size of the reveal—or gap—between the frame and the outer project parts is equal all around. Consistency minimizes the impact of the reveal on the viewer.

With the adhesives on the part, put it in place and apply pressure to it with your fingertips or (for larger parts) with your palm. The goal is to squeeze the hotmelt as thin as possible. Be careful not to move the part as you press down while waiting for the adhesive to set up.

Hotmelt adhesive is particularly useful for gluing large, thin (3/8" thick or thinner) parts, which tend to warp. Because the hotmelt adhesive acts like a clamp, it holds a slightly cupped part flat until the wood glue sets up.

To speed the bonding process when applying parts with wood glue alone, use this technique. Apply a few drops of wood glue to the back of the part, put the part in place to transfer the glue to the backing, and remove the part and let the glue set up until it feels tacky (a few minutes). Then return the part to its place. This approach creates a more secure bond.

We rarely glue parts to each other because it restricts our ability to adjust the spacing between them as we attach the project to its backing. Edge-gluing can add strength to vulnerable parts, however, holding them in place more securely. You can also use edge-gluing to bond selected sections of a project together before tracing the outline of the project onto the backing. To edge-glue parts, use hotmelt adhesive.

Step-by-Step Gluing Guide for the Dolphins

Step 1: Identify Anchor Parts

Study the Dolphins. Identify the key "anchor" parts that will lock in the position of the entire assembly. For the Dolphins, these are the dorsal fins of both dolphins and the lower dolphin's flipper.

Step 2: Attach Upper Dolphin's Dorsal Fin

First glue the upper dolphin's dorsal fin in place (Illus. 9-5). Apply a few drops of wood glue to the back of the part, and then a few drops of hot-melt. Put the dorsal fin in place on the backing and apply pressure to it with your fingertips. Be careful not to move the part as you press down and wait for the glue to set up.

With the first dorsal fin in place, check the spacing between all project parts again and adjust as necessary.

Step 3: Attach Lower Dolphin's Flipper

Next attach the lower dolphin's flipper, repeating the gluing sequence in Step 2.

Illus. 9-5. The dorsal fin of the upper dolphin is a key "anchor" part. Glued in place first, it helps you position the other parts accurately later. Use both wood glue (the "white" dots in the photograph) and hotmelt adhesive (applied with a gun) for a secure bond.

Step 4: Attach Lower Dolphin's Dorsal Fin

Glue down the lower dolphin's dorsal fin, again using a combination of hotmelt and wood glue as described in Step 2.

With the three anchor parts glued in place, you've established the position of all the other parts. As you pick up and glue each remaining part, unglued parts may shift position a bit, but you can easily realign them now that the anchor parts are permanently attached.

Step 5: Edge-Glue Selected Interior Parts

To add stability to the white belly parts, apply hotmelt adhesive to the upper edge of the belly parts and glue them to the dark body (Illus. 9-6) before gluing the body to the backing. Check all the spacing carefully before committing yourself.

Step 6: Glue All Remaining Parts

To attach the remainder of the parts to the backing, use only wood glue. Since the dorsal fin of each dolphin is a vulnerable part, you might put a few drops of hotmelt along the edge of each dorsal fin

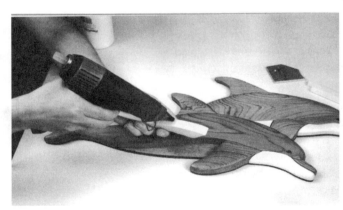

Illus. 9-6. Some parts can be edge-glued to each other with hotmelt adhesive for a more secure bond. For the Dolphins, you might edge-glue the white belly parts to the body.

where it meets each dolphin's body immediately before gluing the body to the backing.

Step 7: Remove Excess Glue

With all the parts glued down, give the glue time to set up. Then check the outside edges of the project to see if any glue oozed onto the backing. If it did, scrape off the excess.

Signing the Project

I sign an intarsia project using a dark brown felt-tipped permanent marker (Illus. 9-7), just before applying the final coat Then, when I apply the final matte spray finish to the project, it seals in the signature.

Be sure to test first that your finish will cover the marker without smudging.

Illus. 9-7. Sign an intarsia project before applying the final coat of finish. A dark brown permanent marker works well.

Summary of Gluing Sequence

1. Assemble all the parts on the backing.
2. Check everything for fit and space all parts as evenly as possible. Use a dark brown marker to stain the backing behind any wide gaps.
3. Starting at the outer edge of the project, identify a few key parts that will anchor the project (keep it from sliding around) while you glue the remainder of the parts. Apply a combination of hotmelt adhesive and wood glue to the anchor parts, one by one, and attach them to the backing.
4. Using wood glue only, attach the interior parts. Avoid flooding them with the glue. Keep glue dots about 1" apart (closer on very small parts).
5. When all parts are glued in place and have set up, check all edges for oozing adhesive. Scrape it away.
6. Sign the project.

Materials List for Dolphins

1. Bottle of yellow wood glue
2. Hotmelt adhesive sticks and application gun
3. Dark brown felt-tipped permanent marker

Chapter 10

Final Finishing

Final Finishing

It's almost time to celebrate your accomplishment! Attaching the hanger and applying the final matte finish (if you choose to do so) are all that remain to finish your intarsia project.

Selecting a Hanger

To hang free-form projects like the Dolphins, we have used two types of hangers over the years: sawtooth hangers and framer's loops. Both are shown in Illus. 10-1.

Caution: When applying a hanger to an intarsia project, always cover the work surface with something soft (a towel or a piece of foam) before turning the project face down on it. Otherwise, you may dent or scratch the face.

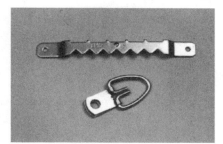

Illus. 10-1. Sawtooth hangers (top) and framer's loops (bottom) both work well for hanging intarsia projects.

Sawtooth Hanger

Probably the most popular with intarsia buffs, the sawtooth hanger is available almost anywhere. These hangers come with their own nails (actually, brads), which you hammer into the back of the project to attach the hanger to it. I've found, however, that hammering the back of an intarsia project can cause parts to pop off. So I use another method to fasten a sawtooth hanger to the back of a project.

Using a hand staple gun, I shoot one or more staples over the nail hole at each end of the hanger (Illus. 10-2). This eliminates the repeated tapping and pounding that can pop parts loose and damage the front of the project. The staples hold the hanger in place as well as—if not better than—nails. If by chance the stapler does not drive the staple tight against the hanger, I gently tap it snug with a tack hammer.

Illus. 10-2. Attach a sawtooth hanger to the back of an intarsia piece with staples, rather than nails. The pounding needed to drive nails can pop parts off the front of the project.

Framer's Loop

My favorite hanger is the type professional framing shops use on pictures. These hangers are available in several sizes at framing shops or in the hardware sections of discount retailers. For projects weighing 20 pounds or less, I use the smallest size. I fasten the hanger to the backing with a small No. 6 x 1/2" roundhead screw (Illus. 10-3). Always predrill a hole for the screw and before drilling, check the intarsia part on the front side of the screw site to be sure that it is thick enough to accept the screw without its point showing.

Marking the Spot for the Hanger

To determine where to attach the hanger to an intarsia project, hold the project between your thumb and index finger (Illus. 10-4) and move it left and right until it hangs the way you want it to. (Be careful not to dig your thumbnail into the soft wood.) With a pencil, make a mark at the center of the end of your finger (Illus. 10-5).

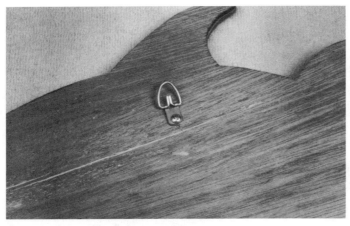

Illus. 10-3. *Use a screw to attach a framer's loop to an intarsia project. Be sure the part on the front opposite the screw is thick enough to accept the screw. Predrill the screw hole.*

Since a sawtooth hanger has several teeth, you can adjust right or left when you hang the project on a nail. The framer's loop also allows for some adjustment. After snugging the screw against the hanger, put the loop on a nail and check how the project hangs. To adjust the loop, loosen the screw and rotate the hanger one direction or the other. Resnug the screw and check again.

Applying the Matte Finish Coat

As explained in Chapter 7, if you prefer a matte finish, as we do, now is the time to apply it. (If you like the gloss finish of the wiping gel, skip this step.)

Hang your intarsia project in a well-ventilated area. Protect the wall or surface behind it with paper or some other covering. Spray a light, even coat of matte finish (see Buyer's Guide) over the entire project. Be sure to follow proper precautions when applying the spray finish. As shown in Illus. 10-6, I wear a respirator even in a well-ventilated area.

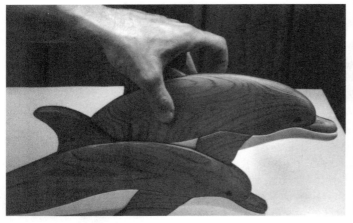

Illus. 10-4. *To determine where to position the hanger, hold the project between your thumb and index finger until it hangs as you want it to.*

Illus. 10-5. *Mark the location for the hanger—at the center of the tip of your finger.*

Let the finish dry thoroughly (10 minutes should do it). Your new intarsia project is ready to hang and enjoy. Congratulations!

Illus. 10-6. Always wear a ventilator when applying spray finishes. Work in a well-ventilated area.

Summary of Hanger Application and Finishing Sequence

1. Find and mark the location for the hanger.
2. Put something soft on your work surface, turn your intarsia project over on it, and attach the hanger of your choice.
3. Optional: Hang the project up, apply a light coat of matte finish, and let it dry thoroughly.

Materials List for Dolphins

1. Hanger of your choice (sawtooth or framer's loop)
2. Appropriate fasteners and other tools for the hanger:
    a. Sawtooth hanger: staple gun and staples; tack hammer (optional)
    b. Framer's loop: drill, No. 6 x 1/2" roundhead screw, screwdriver
3. Spray can of clear matte finish (see Buyer's Guide) (optional)

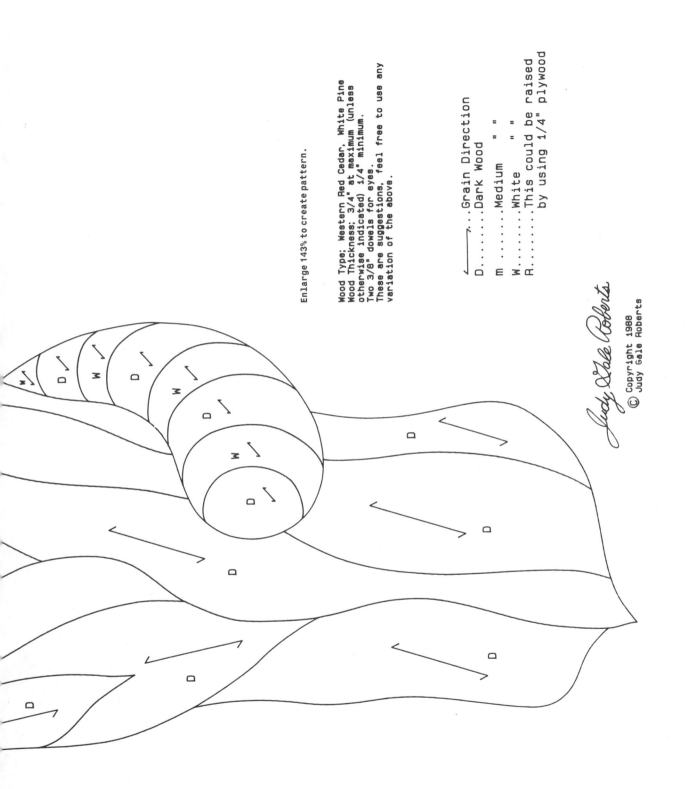

Enlarge 143% to create pattern.

Wood Type: Western Red Cedar, White Pine
Wood Thickness: 3/4" at maximum (unless
otherwise indicated) 1/4" minimum.
Two 3/8" dowels for eyes.
These are suggestions, feel free to use any
variation of the above.

⌐...Grain Direction
D........Dark Wood
m........Medium " "
W........White " "
R........This could be raised
         by using 1/4" plywood

Judy Gale Roberts

Typical patterns for raised areas, cut approx. 1/16" less that the parts to be raised.
You can use these patterns to trace on your plywood for the raised areas.

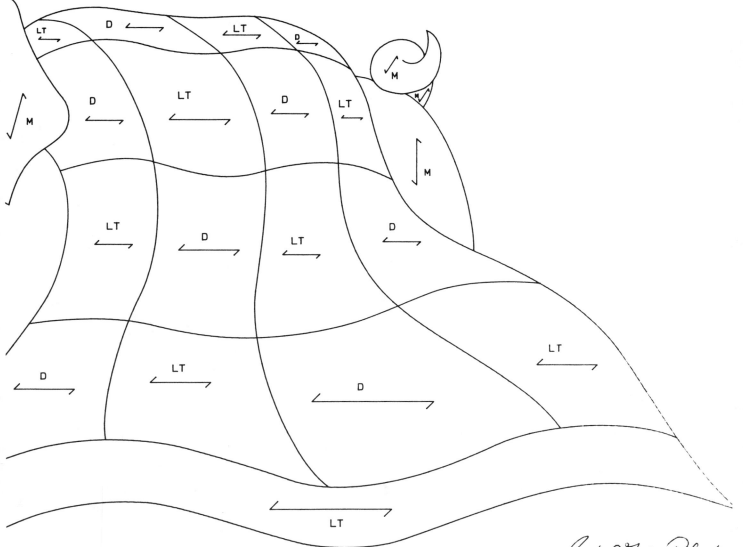

Wood Type; Western
Red Cedar
Wood Thickness; 3/4"
at maximum (unless
otherwise indicated) 1/4"
minimum. These are
suggestions, feel free
to use any variation of
the above.
You will need two 1/2"
dowels approx. 3/4" long
for the nose.

Grain Direction
D...........Dark Wood
MD.........Medium Dark
M...........Medium
LT.........Light
W...........White pine, or any white wood.
R...........This could be raised by using 1/4" plywood.

Rx2.........This could be raised twice, using 1/4" plywood (raising a total of 1/2")
Rx3.........This could be raised three times, using 1/4
plywood (raising a total of 3/4")

Enlarge 143% to create pattern

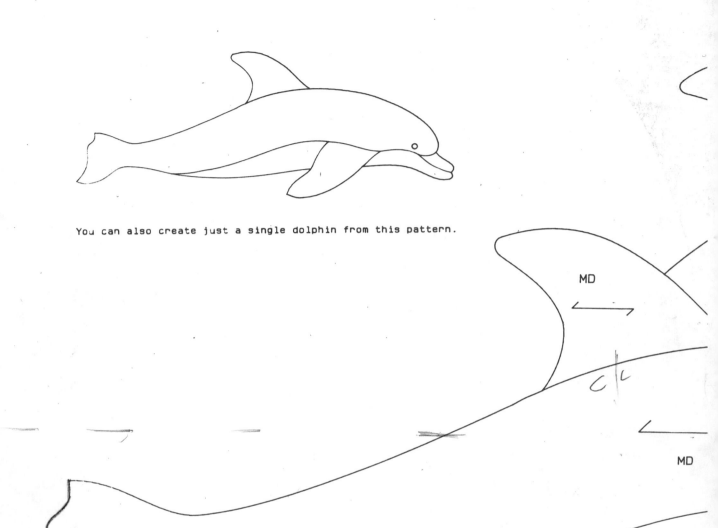

You can also create just a single dolphin from this pattern.

The following are recommendations that I would use for
this project. Feel free to try different mixes of wood tones,
wood types, and grain directions. These patterns were
designed with 3/4" wood in mind, however, any thickness
will work.

You will need two 1/4" dowels cut approx. 3/4" long for the eyes.

Enlarge 143% to create pattern.

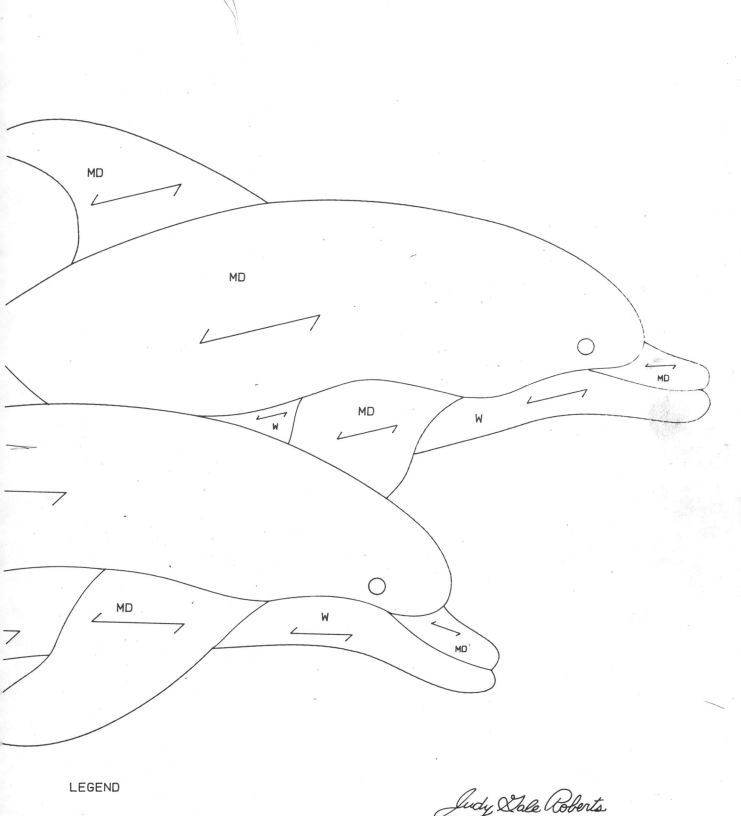

MD

MD

MD

MD

W

MD

W

W

MD

MD

LEGEND

⟶ ..Grain Direction
MD...........Medium Dark shade of wood
W............White pine, or any white wood

You can simplify this pattern by drawing all the parts on white wood and staining the different sections in festive colors, or use a combination of the natural wood and stains. I mix up my own stain by using artist oil paint with a oil based clear sealer (we use Bartley wiping gel).

D

W

MD

W

W

W

LT

m   m

LT

W

W

m

m

m

W

LT

Use a nail (or whatever) to hang your stocking, cover the nail with the angel's hand. Then it will look like the angel is holding the stocking.

W

Fabric (store bought) stocking.

I burned the dowels (after shaping) for the eyes, noses and buttons. The dowels on the boots remain natural.

The following are recommendations that I would use for this project. I use Western Red Cedar, feel free to try different mixes of wood tones, wood types, and grain direction. These patterns were designed with 3/4" wood in mind. However, any thickness will work. *You will need six 3/16" dowels for eyes, four 1/8" dowels for noses and horse eye, five 3/8" dowels for buttons, and two 5/8" dowels for boots, all cut approximately 3/4" in length.*

Enlarge 143% to create pattern.

L E G E N D

⟶ ....Grain Direction
D ....Dark shade of wood
MD ....Medium Dark shade of wood
M.....................Medium shade of wood
LT ....Light shade of wood
W ....White pine, or any white wood

Enlarge 143% to create pattern.

The following are recommendations that I would use for this project. I use Western Red Cedar, feel free to try different mixes of wood tones, wood types, and grain direction. These patterns were designed with 3/4" wood in mind. However, any thickness will work. *You will need six 3/16" dowels for eyes, four 1/8" dowels for noses and horse eye, five 3/8" dowels for buttons, and two 5/8" dowels for boots, all cut approximately 3/4" in length.*

L E G E N D

←——→ .... Grain Direction
D .... Dark shade of wood
MD .... Medium Dark shade of wood
M .... Medium shade of wood
LT .... Light shade of wood
W .... White pine, or any white wood

Enlarge 143% to create pattern.

The following are recommendations that I would use for this project. I use Western Red Cedar, feel free to try different mixes of wood tones, wood types, and grain direction. These patterns were designed with 3/4" wood in mind. However, any thickness will work. *You will need six 3/16" dowels for eyes, four 1/8" dowels for noses and horse eye, five 3/8" dowels for buttons, and two 5/8" dowels for boots, all cut approximately 3/4" in length.*

L E G E N D

→........	Grain Direction
D	Dark shade of wood
MD	Medium Dark shade of wood
M	Medium shade of wood
LT	Light shade of wood
W	White pine, or any white wood

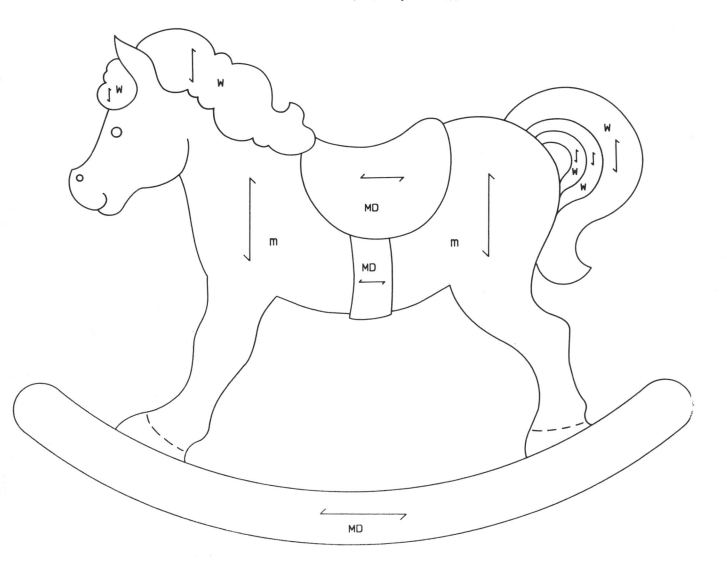

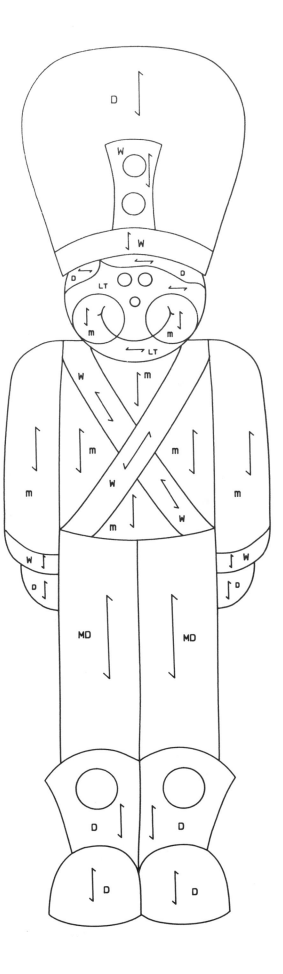

Enlarge 143% to create pattern.

The following are recommendations that I would use for this project. I use Western Red Cedar, feel free to try different mixes of wood tones, wood types, and grain direction. These patterns were designed with 3/4" wood in mind. However, any thickness will work. *You will need six 3/16" dowels for eyes, four 1/8" dowels for noses and horse eye, five 3/8" dowels for buttons, and two 5/8" dowels for boots, all cut approximately 3/4" in length.*

LEGEND

⟶ .... Grain Direction
D .... Dark shade of wood
MD .... Medium Dark shade of wood
M .... Medium shade of wood
LT .... Light shade of wood
W .... White pine, or any white wood

Chapter R1 The Raccoon

Wood Selection and Layout

The Raccoon: Wood Selection and Layout

The following chapters explain step by step how to complete the free-form intarsia Raccoon shown in Illus. R1-1. Especially if you are new to intarsia, please read Chapters 1-10 before beginning the Raccoon. The general information about each intarsia step and detailed explanations of techniques contained in Chapters 1-10 are not repeated in these instructions for the Raccoon.

Illus. R1-1. This free-form Raccoon uses three different wood colors: white, medium, and dark. Here, an extra-dark piece of wood was used to cut the tail, ear, and mask parts, to provide more contrast with the branches.

Preparing the Pattern

Enlarge the Raccoon Pattern at the end of this book and then trace the enlargement to make a pattern for the project.

Use a red felt-tipped pen to trace the enlarged pattern on transparent tracing paper, marking wood color and grain direction on each pattern part. (The arrows on the pattern show grain direction; letters indicate wood color.)

Planning the Approach

Study the pattern and develop a plan of action. Note:

- the wood colors called for

- areas that should be cut from wood thinner than 3/4" (there are none in this particular project)

- raised areas that could be cut from thicker wood rather than shimmed (there are four raised parts on the raccoon's face)

- areas that can be stack-cut (the raccoon's tail and ears)

Selecting the Wood

The Raccoon calls for three shades of wood: dark, medium, and white. If you have an extremely dark piece of wood, however, use it for the dark stripes in the tail and the dark mask around the eyes. These areas will then be darker than the tree, providing an exciting color contrast.

Unusual grains can be used to good effect for the raccoon's body. If your supply of wood with exotic grain patterns is limited, cut only the raccoon's arm and forehead from it and cut the rest of the body parts from straighter grained wood. The tree looks good cut either from straight-grained wood or from wood with an unusual grain pattern. Since most of my white wood does not have an obvious grain pattern, I don't spend much time picking out special pieces for a project.

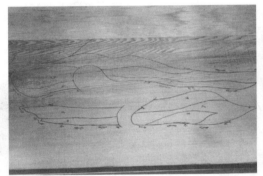

Illus. R1-2. Trace adjoining parts of the pattern that are the same wood color and have the same grain direction without space between them. Number each part as you trace it. The outlines at the bottom are for the left-hand branch; those at the top, for the right-hand branch. Note how the two branches are laid out on separate areas of the board, using two different grain patterns for visual interest.

Laying Out the Project

Transfer the pattern outlines to the wood. Decide which part(s) to transfer first, place that section of the pattern on the wood, and line up the grain direction arrows. If adjoining parts are the same color and have the same grain direction, trace them at one time (to be cut apart during sawing). Use this approach for the branches in this project (Illus. R1-2). Otherwise, leave space between parts as you trace their outlines onto the wood.

Hold the pattern in place around its edges with pushpins. Slide carbon paper under it, smooth it out, and put more pushpins around the part you're ready to trace. As you trace each part, give it a number; this turns the pattern into a map to follow in putting the project together. After you trace each part, remove a few pins and check to be sure you completed the entire outline (Illus. R1-3).

Illus. R1-3. Check the outline of each part after you trace it by removing only a few pushpins.

On free-form projects like the Raccoon, mark parts along the exposed outer edges of the project with arrows to show that no parts fit against them. The arrows tell you that you can relax a bit when sawing these outlines. A line perpendicular to an arrow (Illus. R1-4) indicates where to start relaxing. As an aid for accurate sawing, extend part outlines as though drawing the adjacent part (Illus. R1-5). These lead lines give you time to line up the saw blade before reaching the exacting part of the cut.

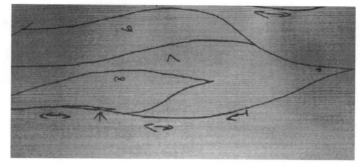

Illus. R1-4. Arrows outside the outlines of Parts 7 and 8 show that they form the outer edge of the project. The line at right angles to the arrow outside Part 7 means "start relaxing here."

If your pen drifts off the outline as you trace it, mark the good side of the line with an arrow (Illus. R1-6).

The white and dark tail parts and the white and dark ear parts of the Raccoon can be stack-cut to ensure a good fit. (It's not mandatory, however.) To do the layout so that you can stack-cut these parts, draw the outlines for all the tail and ear parts on a piece of white wood. Saw off most of the excess white wood around the outlines (cut a blank), put the light blank on top of a dark board, trace the outline of the light blank onto the dark board with a pen, and then cut the darker wood on the outline. When you're ready to saw, you'll put the light blank on top of the dark one (Illus. R1-6), hold the two pieces together with double-sided tape, and saw two identical copies of each part—one from light wood and the other from dark. When the parts are cut out, assemble the appropriately colored ones to match the pattern. (Remove the tape immediately after sawing; the longer it stays on, the harder it is to remove.)

When you've traced and checked the outlines of every part for the Raccoons, it's time to go to the saw.

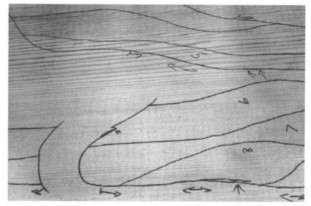

Illus. R1-5. The outlines at the top of Part 6 and on the parts to its left were extended as though tracing the adjacent part. These lead lines let you line up the saw blade before it reaches the sensitive part of the cut. Also note the arrow marking the correct side of the double line to follow.

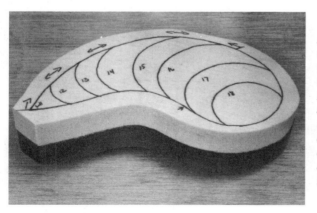

Illus. R1-6. The tail parts of the Raccoon are ready for stack-cutting, to ensure that the alternating dark and light segments will fit together accurately during assembly. For a stack-cut, do the layout on the lighter of the two woods.

Chapter R2 The Raccoon

Sawing

The Raccoon: Sawing

With the outlines of all parts for the Raccoon transferred to the wood, it's time to do the saw work. Be sure to read Chapter 4 for basic sawing techniques and tips before starting to cut out the Raccoon.

Cut Blanks and Drill Holes

Cut the boards on which you traced your parts into blanks, as shown in Illus. R2-1. Also drill a 3/8" diameter hole in each dark mask part for the raccoon's eyes.

Illus. R2-1. Cut the laid-out Raccoon parts into blanks of a manageable size.

Begin at the Band Saw

To saw the parts for the Raccoon, first use the band saw to cut the outlines of major segments of the project. Then separate the interior parts using a scroll saw. I suggest cutting the interior parts apart on a scroll saw because, running a thin No. 2 blade, the scroll saw will remove much less wood than a band saw, with its thicker blade. The scroll saw therefore produces a better (tighter) fit between the interior parts than does the band saw.

If you don't have a scroll saw, you can of course use your band saw, with the thinnest blade you're comfortable running.

As you saw, remember to use an emery-covered sanding block to remove the burr on the bottom of each blank after you make a cut. This is particularly important when you return the piece to the saw table to make a second cut.

Saw Outline of Tree Trunk and Right-Hand Branch

Let's start by cutting the outline of the tree trunk and right-hand branch. (I like to begin sawing on a simple part, to get my motor running.) First I look at the parts to identify any problem areas. I spot one right away.

Note the point where the left-hand branch joins the right branch (the place between Parts 1 and 2 that the pen is pointing to in Illus. R2-2). You can't turn the saw on that point to continue the cut. You'd have to back the blade out of the cut before going any farther.

Backing the saw blade out of a cut, especially a curved cut, can be troublesome. If the cut closes behind the saw blade, you'll have a hard time backing the blade out and may have to scrap the entire part. Even if the cut does not close, it's still very difficult to keep the saw blade on the cutting line while backing it out; you're likely to gouge the side of the part.

To play it safe, spot back-out areas before you begin to cut and then make what I call an escape cut.

Here's the procedure. In waste wood, saw the escape cut to within

---

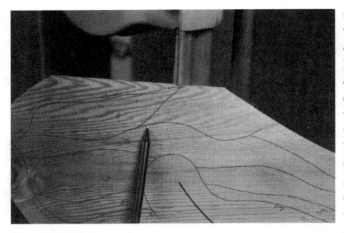

Illus. R2-2. *It's impossible to cut the outline of Parts 1 and 2 in a single pass because you can't turn the saw blade at the point shown by the pen.*

about 1/8" of the layout line at the point where you would have to back the saw out (Illus. R2-3). Then cut along the outline of the part to the point where its layout line intersects the end of your escape cut. (As you approach the point where your cut intersects the escape cut, slow the rate of feed and let the saw blade relax before stopping it.) Then carefully back the saw blade out of the cut about 1/4" and turn it into the escape cut (Illus. R2-4). Once you have cut into the escape cut, you will be able to pull the blank (the good wood containing the part) safely away from the blade without worrying about gouging the part. When planning an escape cut, make sure that the drop-out piece between the good part and the escape cut is tapered like a wedge of pie. (Illus. R2-4 shows this clearly.) This makes the piece easy to remove and eliminates the chance that it might become wedged in, causing another problem. Sand the burr off the bottom of the blank, return it to the saw table, and complete the other saw cut into the intersection (Illus. R2-5).

Now finish cutting around the exterior of the tree trunk and right-hand branch. When you're done, you'll have one large part containing six interior parts. I put this multiple-part piece aside and cut the individual parts from it later with the scroll saw.

Saw Outlines of Two Sections for Left-Hand Branch

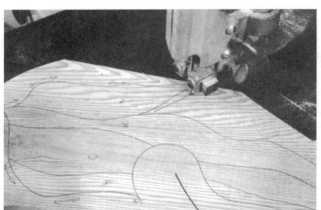

Illus. R2-3. *To cut the outline of Part 2, first saw an escape cut like this one in the adjacent waste wood. Stop the saw 1/8" from the point where the escape cut would intersect the outline of the part.*

Sawing the exterior outline only, cut out the lower section of the left-hand branch, and then the section of the left-hand branch above the coon's arm. Lay these multiple-part pieces aside with the one for the right-hand branch, to saw into individual parts later on the scroll saw.

Saw Outline of Coon's Forehead

Look at the areas on the coon's forehead where the white ear parts fit (Illus. R2-6). These "notches" are only about 1/8" wide. If you are cutting the Raccoon only with a scroll saw running a thin blade, you'll be able to make the two turns in the bottom of each notch and exit without any problem. If you are using a band saw with a 1/8" wide blade, however, the notch is about as wide as the blade, making it difficult to saw.

To saw an area like this on a band saw, use a technique I call scraping. Cut along the outline on one side of the notch, stopping just shy of the "bottom" of the notch. Cut the outline on the other side, also stopping just shy of the end (Illus. R2-7), but this time back the saw blade out a tad and

---

then saw over to the other cut outline (Illus. R2-8)—just like you did when you used the escape cut to saw the outline of the branch. Only a little point of wood will remain in the notch.

With the face of the saw blade, slowly chop this section out, leaving the layout line showing. Using the face of the blade again, lightly touch the bottom of the notch, scraping the blade to the opposite side, until the layout line is removed. It usually takes three or four passes to completely remove the line with this scraping technique (Illus. R2-9). Repeat the process for the other ear notch (Illus. R2-10); then saw the remainder of the outline for the forehead. When you approach the nose section with the inside corner where the white eyebrow meets the forehead, don't worry about sawing an escape cut. Just saw the short segment of the outline first, slowly and carefully back out of the cut, and then make the longer cut from the outside of the forehead into the nose corner.

Illus. R2-4. Back the saw out just a little and then saw toward the escape cut. Plan the location of the escape cut so that the waste piece is tapered like a wedge.

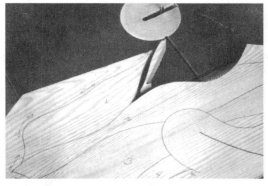

Illus. R2-5. Sawing the outline of the adjacent part removes the final sliver of waste and produces a clean outline.

Saw Outline of Mouth and Cheeks

If you are cutting the Raccoon with only a band saw and are running a 1/8" blade, check the tight curved area where the nose will go with a 1/2" diameter gauge (Illus. R2-11) to see if you will be able to saw it later without a problem. If you enlarged the pattern as Judy suggested in Chapter R1, the radius of the area should be larger than the plug—meaning that you can cut it on your band saw. If you have a scroll saw, you'll be cutting the nose section out later on it.

Cut along the outline of the mouth and cheeks, leaving the interior parts uncut for now. It makes no difference where you begin to saw this outline. The area where the mouth joins the two cheek parts will be fragile; be careful there. With the outline cut, lay this multiple-part piece aside to be cut apart later on the scroll saw.

Stack-Cut the Tail Outline

Tape together the two wood layers for the tail, white layer on the top, with double-sided tape. (Wait until immediately before cutting the tail outline to tape the layers together, and untape them as soon as possible after sawing the tail segments apart. One hour is about the longest you should leave the pieces taped together. Therefore, you want to stack-cut the tail outline last and then cut the interior parts of the tail apart first when you go to the scroll saw.)

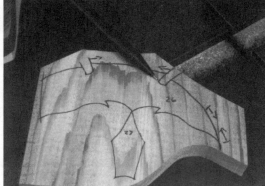

Illus. R2-6. These notches for the raccoon's ears are only 1/8" wide, making them difficult to cut with a band saw.

The tail outline, with its smooth, flowing lines, is very easy to cut. Stack-cutting through a double thickness of the wood makes squareness of the sides more critical, however. Be sure to check the edges for squareness after cutting the outline. If they are quite a bit out of square, you will have fit problems with your parts. You may want to retrace the parts and recut them.

Move to the Scroll Saw

Now move to the scroll saw to cut all the multiple-part segments (Illus. R2-12) into individual parts. Deburr the bottoms of all blanks first using an emery-covered sanding block.

Start with the raccoon's tail. Begin sawing at the small end of the tail, so you will have something to hold onto as you cut off successive segments (Illus. R2-13). After you've sawed the segments apart, remove the tape and separate the white and dark tail parts right away.

Continue sawing each of the multiple-part pieces into their individual parts—until all the Raccoon parts are cut out.

Now you're ready to check the fit of everything and trim any parts that need it.

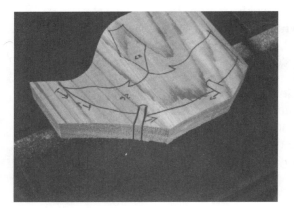

Illus. R2-7. To cut the notches, first saw the outlines on both sides of the notch, stopping just shy of the end.

Illus. R2-8. At the end of the second cut, back out the saw blade and saw to the first cut, using that cut like an escape cut. Note the small amount of wood remaining at the bottom of the notch.

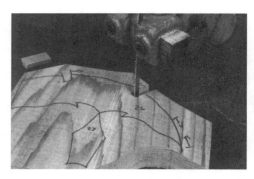

Illus. R2-9. Using the face of the saw blade, "scrape" away the waste, first stopping just short of the layout line and then removing it.

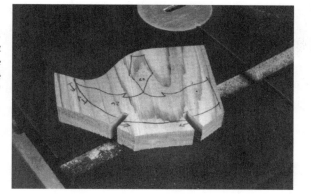

Illus. R2-10.
Scraping with a band saw blade produced these clean 1/8" notches.

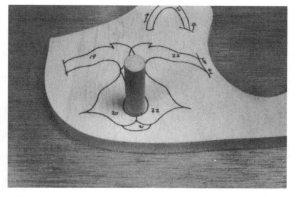

Illus. R2-11. Since the curve of the raccoon's nose is larger than this 1/2" diameter plug, the outline of the nose can be cut successfully on a band saw running a 1/8" blade. If you have a scroll saw, however, use it for the interior cuts.

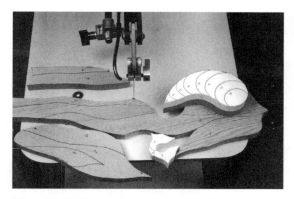

Illus. R2-12. The outlines of these multi-part segments for the Raccoon were cut on a band saw. If you have a scroll saw, use it to separate the individual parts in each segment. The scroll saw's thinner blade produces a tighter fit between the interior parts.

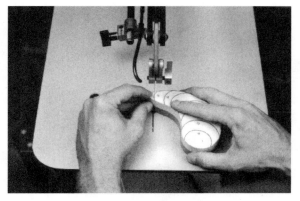

Illus. R2-13. To cut the segments of the stack-cut tail, begin with the smallest one. You'll have more wood to hold onto with this approach. Remove the double-sided tape between the two colors immediately after sawing.

Chapter R3 The Raccoon

Checking the Fit

The Raccoon: Checking the Fit

Use sandpaper to remove any burrs on the edges of the Raccoon parts. Then transfer the part number on the front of each part to its back.

Assembling and Checking Part Fit

Now lay out the Raccoon parts on top of the pattern and take a close look at each of them. Look for parts that fit too tightly, parts with a large gap on one side and almost no space on the other, and parts whose edges are seriously out of square. Layout lines remaining on the parts can indicate inaccurately cut outlines.

On the parts that need it, carefully mark areas to be trimmed. Use the saw (or sand if you can keep the edges of the parts square) to trim these parts. Put each one back in place and recheck it after trimming (Illus. R3-1).

If a part simply won't fit after repeated attempts to trim it, recut the part.

Previewing and Planning

Using some double-sided tape, attach the Raccoon to a scrap board. Stand it up and give it a good overall look. (Or lay the Raccoon out on the floor and then step back from it.)

Catch a second wind. Take time to check how the wood colors and grains work together. Plan your approach to sanding and shaping, the next step. Think about which parts should be thinner than others and which should be thicker—that is, which parts of the Raccoon are the farthest from the viewer and which are the closest. Also think about texture and dimension.

If you decide that a part is too light or dark, cut a replacement now.

Illus. R3-1. All the Raccoon parts have been trimmed and are laid out on the pattern for a final check before sanding and shaping.

Chapter R4 The Raccoon

Sanding and Shaping

The Raccoon: Sanding and Shaping

With all the Raccoon parts trimmed to size, you're ready to polish the look of the project—adding dimension to and defining the shape of the parts. Use the sander of your choice: belt, disc, pneumatic drum, or flexible drum. See Chapter 6 for general sanding and shaping tips before you begin.

Preparing to Sand
Research the Subject

Look at pictures of raccoons and familiarize yourself with their characteristics. As you shape the Raccoon parts, refer to the picture of the finished project (Illus. R1-1 on page 107 in Chapter R1) as well as the photographs throughout this chapter. Pay attention to the thickness relationships between the parts, note how the parts are tapered, and look at how their edges are rounded or shaped.

Keep these visual references and the laid-out Raccoon parts close to your sanding area, so you can check progress as you sand and shape each part and mark sanded thicknesses on the edges of unsanded parts.

Cut Temporary Sanding Backings

Study the Raccoon to identify parts that can be sanded as one. Unit-sanding saves time and produces a more attractive result in some areas than rounding the edges of each part.

The Raccoon has two areas that benefit from unit-sanding: the face and the tail. Cut temporary sanding backings for these areas from scrap plywood (Illus. R4-1) now. When you're ready to sand them, attach the parts to the backing with double-sided tape. (Trace the outline for the backing from the pattern or lay out the parts on the backing material and trace around them. See Chapter 6 for complete instructions.)

You can also sand all the tree parts as one if you wish, but I prefer to sand the parts individually. Sanding these parts one by one lets you vary the angles of the branch sections, which adds texture to the tree.

Make Shims for Raised Areas

The central face parts (nose and cheeks) of the Raccoon are designed to be raised above the surrounding face parts. They are marked with an "R" on the pattern.

While you have the scrap plywood out to cut the temporary sanding backings, also cut

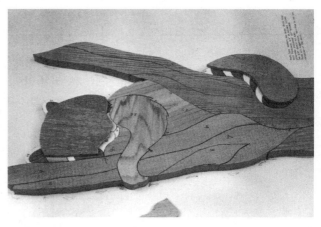

Illus. R4-1. Cut temporary sanding backings from scrap plywood so that you can sand the head and the tail parts of the Raccoon as units. In this illustration, the backings are on top of the areas, so that you can see them.

Illus. R4-2. To raise the four nose and cheek parts 1/4", as the Raccoon pattern instructs, cut a plywood shim (like the one shown here) just a hair smaller than the parts.

a shim to raise these parts. Make the shim a little smaller than the outline of the parts (Illus. R4-2). (If, earlier, you cut the nose and cheek parts from wood thicker than 3/4", you won't need a shim for them.)

When you've cut the shim, put it in place under the parts in your layout (Illus. R4-3).

Rough-Sanding

All the Raccoon parts are 3/4" thick—except the raised areas, which with their shim are 1" thick. Now rough-sand the parts to make some parts thinner than the others. Remember, just rough in the thicknesses on this pass. Don't spend too much time perfecting each part.

The sanding work on the Raccoon is more challenging that that required for the Dolphins. For example, some parts of the Raccoon should be tapered so that they are thicker on one side than on the other. No doubt, you'll need to resand some parts to adjust their thicknesses or their edge treatment as you work your way through the project. So just rough-sand until you establish all the thickness levels you want. Rounding the edges is of secondary concern at this point; focus your attention on establishing good thickness relationships between the various parts.

Note: The terms right and left are used throughout this chapter to describe the location of parts. In these explanations, the right (or left) side of the Raccoon is the side of the project on the viewer's right (or left).

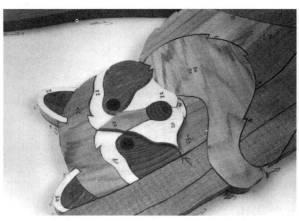

Illus. R4-3. Note how the shim raises the nose and cheeks above the surrounding parts.

The Raccoon's Body Parts

Following the rule of perspective, areas of the project farthest away from the viewer should be the thinnest; those closest to the viewer should be the thickest. Since the raccoon is behind the tree branches, its two body parts—the one below the chin and the one below the arm—should be the thinnest parts of the project. Sand these parts down to a thickness of 3/8", slightly rounding the raccoon's back toward its outer edge (Illus. R4-4).

Put the rough-sanded body parts back in the layout and, with a mechanical pencil, mark their thickness on the edges of the surrounding parts (under the chin, around the arm, and where the body parts touch the tree branches) (Illus. R4-5).

All the Tree Parts

Now sand each of the parts that make up the tree branches. Begin with the branch parts on the right-hand side of the project; then do the parts on the left side. Looking at the Raccoon, note that the branch parts that touch the coon's body need to be thicker than the body (since they are in front of the raccoon). Also note that the branch sections at the lower right need to be thinner than the tail (since the tail wraps around that branch and is therefore closer to the viewer).

Before beginning to sand any of the right-hand branch parts, mark their edges to show where the tail adjoins them (Illus. R4-6). When you sand the edge of a branch part that the tail butts against, it's very important to leave some thickness there. Do not completely round over the edge of the branch. The upper end of the tail (where it comes from behind the branch) needs to be thinner than the branch in front of it.

Upper Right Branch Parts. Start with the outer part of the upper right branch. Taper this part down toward the raccoon's tail to about 3/8" thick, slightly angling it toward its outer edge (Illus. R4-7). When you've roughed in its thickness, put the part back on the layout and mark the thickness on the adjoining branch part (Illus. R4-8).

Now sand the center part of the right-hand branch, angling it down toward the pencil mark on its edge and tapering it to a 3/8" thickness toward the end that adjoins the tail, as you did with the outer branch part. Finally, round the exposed (left) edge of this branch part (Illus. R4-9). Return the sanded part to the layout and mark its thickness on the edge of the adjoining branch part.

Lower Right Branch Parts. Next sand the outer right-hand branch part below the raccoon's tail to a thickness of 3/8", rounding it toward the exposed edge (Illus. R4-10). Again, put the part in place and mark its thickness on the edge of the adjoining branch part.

Now sand the adjoining branch part, angling its right edge to the pencil mark at 3/8" thick. The other side of the part should be thicker—about 1/2". Put the part in place and mark its depth on the lower edge of the adjoining branch part. (The upper edge of that adjoining part—above the raccoon's tail—has already been marked for depth.)

Following the same contour you used for the branch you just sanded, sand the right edge of this branch part (the third one from the right) down to the pencil line (making it about 1/2" thick on its lower right edge), but leave it slightly thicker (approximately 9/16") on its left edge. Then round the edge of the part where it touches the raccoon's body, staying above the pencil line you made there earlier. As you round the upper portion of the branch, follow the contour you established for the other two upper branch parts (Illus. R4-11).

Put the sanded branch part in place and mark its thickness on the edges of all the left-hand branch parts that adjoin it.

Lower Left Branch Parts. Sand the branch part at the bottom left first, tapering it down to the pencil line on its right edge and then rounding it toward its outer edge. Put it in place and mark its depth on the edge of the branch part above it (Illus. R4-12).

You're ready to work on the three-part branch area below the coon's arm. Since the arm crosses in front of the upper edge of these branch

Illus. R4-4. Sand the raccoon's body parts—the areas of the composition farthest away from the viewer—to 3/8" thick. Round the back toward its notched outer edge.

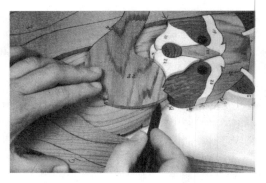

Illus. R4-5. As you reduce the thickness of each part, mark the new thickness on the edges of all adjoining parts to use as a reference when you sand those parts. Do not sand below these edge markings.

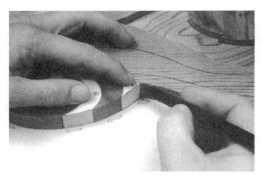

Illus. R4-6. Before sanding the tree branches on the right side of the project, mark their edges to show where the raccoon's tail butts against them.

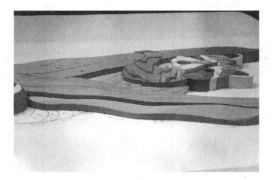

Illus. R4-7. Taper the outer part of the upper right branch down toward the tail to a thickness of 3/8". Slightly angle the part toward its outer edge.

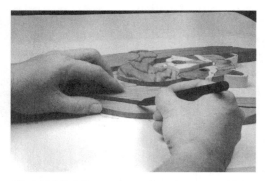

Illus. R4-8. After you sand each part, put it in place and mark its thickness on any adjoining parts.

Illus. R4-9. Taper the central part of the right-hand branch to 3/8" thick where it joins the tail. Angle the edge that adjoins the first branch part down to the pencil line on it. Round the exposed edge of the part.

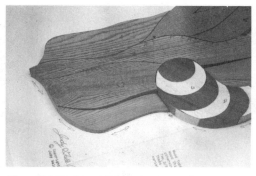

Illus. R4-10. Sand this outer branch part, below the raccoon's tail, to 3/8" thick and then round it toward the exposed edge.

Illus. R4-11. Keep the left side of the central branch part thicker than its right side. Follow the contour of the other branch parts. Round the edge of the part where it touches the raccoon's body, but keep the branch noticeably thicker in that area than the body.

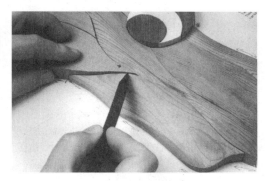

Illus. R4-12. Sand the part at the bottom left of the tree, tapering it to the same thickness as its neighbor to the right. Round its outer edge, and then mark its thickness on the edge of the part above it.

Illus. R4-13. Taper the branch parts below the raccoon's arm thinner (about 1/2" thick) toward the end nearest the arm. Round the inner branch part toward the edge next to the raccoon. Round the outer two parts toward their outer edges. Mark all thicknesses on adjoining parts as you shape these parts.

parts, taper these parts thinner toward their upper edges, to make the coon's arm appear thicker. (Following the same principle, you'll taper the branch parts above the arm thinner at their bottoms.)

Taper the three lower left branch parts to a thickness of about 1/2" where they meet the arm. Round the lower edges of the parts to the pencil lines showing the thickness of the adjoining branch(es). Round the inner edge of the inner branch segment toward the raccoon's body. Round the two outer branch segments toward their outer edges. Continue to mark the edges of adjoining parts as you sand each of these branch parts. Illus. R4-13 shows these branch parts after sanding and shaping.

Upper Left Branch Parts. To determine the thickness of the two branch parts at the upper left, remove the arm part and slide the upper

Illus. R4-14. Slide the parts for the upper and lower left branches together to match the thicknesses of the two. Mark the thickness of the lower parts on the edges of the upper ones.

Illus. R4-15. Gradually taper the ends of the upper branch parts toward the raccoon's arm, being careful not to sand below the thickness markings on their lower edges.

branch sections down to meet the sanded lower branch sections. Mark the thickness of the lower branch sections on the upper sections (Illus. R4-14). Matching the thickness of the upper branch parts with that of the lower parts makes them look more like one single branch.

Sand these parts, gradually tapering them thinner toward the arm, but sanding no lower than the edge markings for the lower branch parts. Be careful not to sand these sections too thin. They should be thicker than the left edge of the coon's head, which you'll sand and shape later. Round the outer left branch part toward its outer edge. Do not round the inner edge of the branch part next to the raccoon's head yet. (You'll round that edge after you have sanded and shaped the face.)

Put the branch parts back in place (Illus. R4-15) and mark the thickness of the inner branch part on the edge of all the parts it touches on the raccoon's head. Also mark the branch thickness on the upper and lower edges of the raccoon's paw.

At this point you could sand the raccoon's arm next, or its tail. Let's do the arm, because it's quicker.

The Arm

Taper the arm thinner toward the coon's head (to make the head appear thicker). But keep in mind that the arm should be thicker than both the coon's body and the tree branch it's wrapped around, so be careful not to sand below any of the pencil lines on its edges. Just rough in the arm thickness, putting the part back in its place often to make sure it's shaping up as you intend. Remember: It's easier to sand more wood off a piece than it is to put wood back on it!

Taper the arm to a thickness of about 1/2" where it meets the head. Then sand the paw area to look like it is wrapped around the tree branch. Use the pencil lines on its edges to follow the contour of the branch parts, but keep the paw 1/4" to 1/8" thicker than the branch (Illus. R4-16).

Then sand a dip in the crook of the coon's arm, staying above the pencil line on its edge marking the thickness of the coon's body (Illus. R4-17). Put the arm in place and mark its thickness on the bottom edge of the coon's head.

The Raccoon's Face

Prepare to Unit-Sand. You'll sand all the face parts (except the dark nose part, the small white chin, and the ears) as one unit, attached with double-sided tape to the temporary sanding backing you cut earlier.

To prepare the face for sanding, first turn the four raised face parts upside down, putting the dark nose part in place temporarily to establish the proper spacing. Find the plywood shim you cut earlier for these raised parts and attach it to the backside of the parts with double-sided tape (Illus. R4-18). (Don't put tape on the dark nose part; remove it once all the other parts are taped to the shim.) You want to sand this raised area with its shim in place so you can blend its edges with the parts around it.

Now assemble all the remaining face parts upside down around the upside-down nose area with the shim attached. Tape all the parts together (Illus. R4-19). Then put the sanding backing on top of the taped parts, press down to affix the tape to the backing, and carefully turn the whole thing right side up. (Because of the difference in levels caused by the shim, some parts might not be securely attached. Press on them to attach them more tightly.)

Rough-Sand and Shape. Take a deep breath and dive in. First sand to blend the raised nose areas with the surrounding parts. Keeping the medium-dark bridge section the thickest, taper the face slightly toward the white cheek areas, making the cheeks 1/16" thinner than the dark bridge of the nose. This emphasizes the nose. Then lower the left side of the raccoon's face, sanding it below the pencil line on its edge to make it thinner than the branch adjoining it. (That edge of the raccoon's head is behind the tree.)

As you sand the lower face, be sure not to sand below the pencil line on the edge. You want the face (head) thicker than the coon's body below the chin. Taper the sides and the top of the raccoon's face toward the outside edges (Illus. R4-20). Round the forehead back almost to the exposed edge. Leave the right edge of the head a bit more abrupt; don't round it toward the outside.

Clean Up. When you're satisfied with the basic shape and contouring of the face, clean it up some now. Sand by hand or with a sander using a fine-grit paper—or do a little of both. It's easier to finish-sand the faces of these parts while they are still taped together.

When the parts are exactly the way you want them, remove the tape and place all the face parts back on the layout (Illus. R4-21), putting the shim under the raised nose parts, where it will be glued later.

The Ears, the Nose, the Lips, the Chin

Ears. Mark the thickness of the coon's forehead on the lower edges of the dark ear parts. Taper the edges toward the pencil line. The thickness at

---

Illus. R4-16. Taper the arm thinner toward the head. Taper the paw to look like it is wrapped around the branch—but make sure it is 1/8" or more thicker than the branch.

Illus. R4-17. Sanding this dip at the bend of the coon's arm adds dimension and realism to the project.

Illus. R4-18. Before assembling the raccoon's face for unit sanding, tape the shim for the area around the nose to the back of those parts. Raised areas like this one should be sanded at their proper height.

Illus. R4-19. Assemble the remaining face parts upside down around the shimmed nose. Use double-sided tape to hold them in place. Position the sanding backing (not shown here) on top of the parts and press down to affix it to the taped parts.

Illus. R4-20. Looking at the coon's head from the edge, note that it is thicker in the center and thinner toward the outer edges. The raised areas have been blended to meet the non-raised parts. Sand the left edge of the face thinner than the branch that adjoins it.

Illus. R4-21. After rough- and finish-sanding, the face shows contouring and contrasts in thickness between the raised nose area (sitting on its shim) and the rest of the parts.

the top of the ears should be about 5/16", tapering to 3/16" where the ears join the head.

Mark the thickness of the dark ear parts on the inner edges of the white parts (Illus. R4-22). Using the pencil line to indicate the angle at which to sand, taper the white wood as you did the dark wood. Sand the white parts to about 1/8" above the pencil line (Illus. R4-23).

Nose. Put the dark nose part in place in the layout and mark around its edges to show the thickness of the white wood cheeks. Slightly round the edges of the nose all around its circumference to the pencil lines (Illus. R4-24).

Lips. Remove the two cheek parts from the layout (you have already sanded these) and round the edges that form the upper lip down toward the mouth (Illus. R4-24). Put the parts back in the layout and mark their thickness on the upper edge of the white chin part.

Chin. Sand the chin, tapering it to the pencil line on its upper edge (Illus. R4-24).

The Inner Branch at Upper Left

With all the sanding completed for the face, mark its thickness on the edge of the inner upper left branch (Illus. R4-25). Now round the edge of the branch toward the head (Illus. R4-26), being careful not to sand below the pencil marking.

The Tail

After completing the face, the tail is a "piece of cake." Turn all the tail parts upside down, put double-sided tape on them, and then cover them with the temporary sanding backing you cut earlier.

Taper the top edge of the tail to a thickness of about 3/16"—to give the illusion that the tail is coming out from behind the tree. Since the lower end of the tail wraps around the front of the tree, it should be the thickest part of the composition. Round the edges on the upper half of the tail to below the pencil lines, but keep the lower edge of the tail thicker than the pencil markings (Illus. R4-27). First sand the tail to establish the angle; then round the edges.

Finish-Sanding

At this point, all the Raccoon parts (except the eyes) are rough-sanded and shaped—and the face is finish-sanded. If you're pleased with the overall shape and thickness of all the parts, start to clean up the project now. Sand the exposed edges to remove any saw marks and soften any roughness, and sand out any deep scratches on the faces of the parts.

Completing the Eyes

Make the coon's eyes the same way you did the Dolphin's (see Chapter 6) but for the Raccoon use a 3/8" diameter dowel.

With the dowel in one piece (it's easier to work with whole), round

Illus. R4-22. After sanding the dark ear parts, put them in place and mark the thickness (about 5/16") on the inner edge of the white ear parts.

Illus. R4-23. The white edges of the ear should be about 1/8" thicker than the dark inner ear parts. Follow the same angle as for the inner ears.

Illus. R4-24. Round the edges of the nose toward the white cheeks, round the lower edges of the cheeks to form the upper lips, and then taper the upper edge of the chin toward the lips.

Illus. R4-25. Mark the thickness of the head on the edge of the branch next to it.

Illus. R4-26. Round the inner edge of the branch next to the coon's head toward the head, keeping it just a bit thicker than the head where the two adjoin.

Illus. R4-27. Sanding all the tail parts as one (attached to the sanding backing with tape), taper the tail down to about 3/16" at the small end. Round the tail down below the pencil line on its upper half but above the pencil line on the lower end. Round the exposed edges toward the outside.

both ends. Use a wood burner with a flat shading tip to darken the ends of the dowel or stain the ends. (Another option is to use a dark walnut dowel.)

Slide the dowel into one of the dark mask parts from the back, so that its rounded surface is slightly raised on the front of the part. Mark the length of the dowel on the back, remove it, and cut the first "eye" to length. Repeat for the second eye.

Put an eye in each mask part (Illus. R4-28), check its length, glue it in place, and cover the glued area with masking tape so you can turn the part right-side up without glue oozing out on your work surface. Let the eyes dry.

That's it! The Raccoon is ready for finishing and assembly.

Illus. R4-28. Round the tip of a 3/8" dowel for each eye. Burn or stain the tip to darken it—or use a walnut dowel.

Chapter R5 The Raccoon

Finishing, Backing and Gluing

The Raccoon: Finishing, Backing, and Gluing

With all the sanding and shaping complete, it's time to apply finish to the Raccoon parts, cut a backing for the project, glue it together, and finally, attach a hanger and spray on a matte finish (optional).

Applying the Finish

With fine sandpaper (preferably a stearate-coated silicon carbide sheet), lightly sand the edges of each part to remove any saw burrs and to gently soften (round) them.

Thoroughly remove sawdust from the parts. Use compressed air or a soft-bristled brush.

Now apply the finish of your choice to the Raccoon parts. Chapter 7 contains step-by-step instructions for applying a three-coat wiping gel finish to an intarsia project.

Let the parts dry thoroughly (preferably overnight), with space between them (Illus. R5-1).

Cutting the Backing

Prepare to cut a backing on which to assemble and glue the Raccoon. Use a piece of 1/4" plywood. (We prefer lauan plywood, for its absence of voids.) Using repositionable spray adhesive, attach a piece of white paper larger than the Raccoon to the front of the plywood. Then spray the surface of the paper lightly with the adhesive, just to make it tacky.

Illus. R5-1. After applying and wiping off the final finish coat, leave space between the parts of the Raccoon when you lay them aside to dry.

Lay out all the Raccoon parts on the paper-covered backing, adjusting the spacing around them exactly as you want it for the finished project. Try to even out the spacing around the parts. This makes gaps less noticeable. To accentuate a line between two parts, leave about 1/16" space between them.

Now use a mechanical pencil to trace the outline of the project (Illus. R5-2). The paper covering the backing keeps the pencil from catching in the surface grain of the plywood and makes the outline easier to see.

Cut the backing just inside the layout line using a band saw. (With the backing a bit smaller than the project, it is less likely to show when the work is glued to it.)

After you've cut the backing, remove its paper covering, sand and stain its edges, and seal its back. See Chapter 8 for complete instructions for each of these activities.

Gluing Down the Parts

Assemble the Raccoon parts on the backing. Work with the parts to even out the spacing around them. Uneven spacing between parts makes the whole project look bad. If you can't adjust parts to eliminate a gap, use a brown marker to darken the backing behind the gap. That makes it less noticeable.

To glue down a free-form project like the Raccoon, start with the outside parts. Examine the Raccoon and identify some anchor parts—outside parts that determine the position of all the others. Use a combination of hotmelt adhesive and wood glue to attach these parts.

Illus. R5-2. With the Raccoon parts assembled on paper-covered backing plywood, trace around them to make an outline on which to cut the backing. Note that all parts are carefully spaced as for the finished piece.

Apply only a few drops of adhesive to each part. Be especially careful not to flood the parts with wood glue; the moisture in it can warp the parts.

The Anchor Parts

Begin by attaching the **outer branch segment at the upper right.** Apply a few dots of wood glue first; then a few dots of hotmelt (Illus. R5-3). Put the part in place carefully and press on it with your fingers until the hotmelt sets up.

Check the spacing around the parts again and adjust it if necessary. (Parts might have shifted slightly when you removed the branch or when you put it in place after applying the glue.) Next glue the **outer branch segment at the lower left** (Illus. R5-4), then the **outer branch segment at the lower right** (Illus. R5-5), and finally the **outer branch segment at the upper left** (Illus. R5-6).

The Interior Parts

Using wood glue only (or a combination of glue and hotmelt if you wish), glue down the interior parts.

First glue down the **branch segment beside the raccoon's head.** Then glue down **all the head parts except the raised ones.** In projects with raised parts, I find it's best to glue down the parts surrounding a raised part first and let the glue on these surrounding parts set up for awhile. (If you use hotmelt on the surrounding parts, you don't have to wait.) When the glue has set up, lift out the raised parts and the shim under them. Apply glue to the shim, put it in place, let it set up, and then glue the raised parts to the shim.

Illus. R5-3. First, glue down the outer segment of the upper right branch. Dot wood glue (white in the photograph) on the back of the part; then apply hotmelt adhesive between the dots.

Illus. R5-4. Second, glue down the lower left branch part, using the wood glue/hotmelt combination. A little glue goes a long way.

Illus. R5-5. Third, glue down the branch on the outside lower right.

Illus. R5-6. The last anchor part is the outer branch on the upper left. When it is glued down, the positions of the interior parts are locked in.

One by one, glue down the **remainder** of the Raccoon parts. Give everything time to dry, and then check the edges of the project to see if any glue has oozed onto the backing. If it has, scrape it off.

Signing the Project and Attaching a Hanger

Sign the Raccoon with a brown felt-tipped permanent marker.

Attach either a sawtooth hanger or a framer's loop to the backside of the Raccoon. See the instructions in Chapter 10.

Applying a Matte Finish

Hang the Raccoon up and spray the project with a matte finish—if you prefer that look. (The matte finish is optional; many people like the gloss finish produced by the wiping gel.)

Buyer's Guide

Buyer's Guide

Essential Tools

Saw: To cut out intarsia parts, we recommend a band saw (12" or 14" model) or a scroll saw (14" at least). It is also possible to use a jigsaw or a coping saw.

Sander: For rounding and shaping, use a belt sander, a disc sander, a combination belt and disc sander, a pneumatic drum sander, a drum sander, or files and rasps. If using a hand-held belt sander, you will need to clamp it to a table. You can purchase a stand for some hand-held belt sanders (see below).

Other Items for Intarsia

Band Saw Accessories:

Blades for Sears 14" Model
1/8" x 15 x 93 ½": Sears Catalog No. 9F 27191
1/4" x 6 x 93 ½": Sears Catalog No. 9F 27192

Composite Resin Blade Guides
"Cool Blocks"
Garrett Wade
161 Avenue of the Americas
NY, NY 10013
(800) 221-2942

Intarsia Patterns (full size):

Roberts Studio
PO Box 1925
Lufkin, TX 75902
(409) 632-9663

Marker:

Sharpie Brown Fine-Point Permanent
Most office supply stores

Moisture Meter:

Delmhorst Instrument Co.
51 Indian Lane East
Towaco, NJ 07082

Sanders and Sandpaper:

Belt Sander

Bosch Model #3270D has an optional
sanding stand with or without a fence
Source: Your local Bosch dealer

Drum Sander

Sand-Rite Manufacturing Co.
321 N. Justine St.
Chicago, IL 60607

"Flex" Drum Sander
Seyco Sales
PO Box 472749
Garland, TX 75047
(800) 462-3353

Nonloading Silicon Carbide Sanding Sheets
Sungold Sandpaper
Trendlines
375 Beacham St.
Chelsea, MA 02150

Wood Finishes:

Bartley Wiping Gel
Seyco Sales
PO Box 472749
Garland, TX 75047
(800) 462-3353 or
The Bartley Co. Ltd.
(800) BARTLEY

Krylon Matte Spray Finish
Dick Blick
PO Box 1267
Galesburg, IL 61401
Order Number 8004-00
(800) 447-8192

INTARSIA PATTERNS available from JUDY GALE ROBERTS

P.O. BOX 1925 • LUFKIN, TX 75902 • (409) 632-9663 • FAX (409) 632-7977

FOR A MORE DETAILED DESCRIPTION WITH PICTURES OF THE FOLLOWING PATTERNS,
PLEASE WRITE OR CALL THE ABOVE ADDRESS .

PANDA	DUCK	UP CARROUSEL
TOUCAN	PIG IN A BLANKET	DOWN CARROUSEL
RACCOON	BAG LADY	CAMEL
CAT IN BAG	CURIOUS COON	ROSE BUD
SEASCAPE	BASS	BARN OWL
ROSE	CAT IN A CHAIR	WABBIT
CAT WITH YARN	BOG BUDDIES	TROPICAL FISH
KOALA BEARS	MANATEE "ENDANGERED SPECIES SERIES"	ANTIQUE SANTA
BIG FOOT CLOWN	POLAR BEAR "ENDANGERED SPECIES SERIES"	CHRISTMAS ORNAMENTS
CLOWN IN WINDOW	TIGER "ENDANGERED SPECIES SERIES"	OH HOOT HAWAIIAN
CLOWN WITH DAISIES	ELEPHANT "ENDANGERED SPECIES SERIES"	ROCKY TOP
BUCK DEER	BLACK RHINO "ENDANGERED SPECIES SERIES"	CALLAS FLOWER
HORSE	SANTA	FLORIDA PANTHER
BUTTERFLY AND ORCA	WREATH	MOOSE
OH HOOT WEST	DOLPHIN	GIRAFFE
MOUSE	PENGUINS	COYOTE
CHRISTMAS STOCKINGS	DOG	STILL POTTERY
PELICAN	U S A EAGLE	WOLF
HOBO CLOWN	COW	OL' BLUE
FLAMINGOS	BEARS	FAWN AND DOE
STILL LIFE	SWAN	WHITE TAIL DEER
LIGHT HOUSE	SAIL BOAT	CHRISTMAS SIGN
BALLOON	ARIZONA	ANGEL

**THE PATTERNS ABOVE ARE PRINTED FULL SIZE ON 17 1/2" x 23" TRANSPARENT TRACING PAPER,
EACH PATTERN COMES WITH A 8" x 10" BLACK AND WHITE PRINT OF THE FINISHED PROJECT.
THE PATTERNS ABOVE SELL FOR $5.95 EACH OR 3 FOR $15.95**

EAGLE	WOODLAND TRAIL	SEA GULL PILING
CLOUD NINE	EAGLE LANDING	BUFFALO
LAST SUPPER	INDIAN	ON A LIMB COON
	OWL	

**THE PATTERNS ABOVE ARE PRINTED FULL SIZE ON 25" x 38" TRANSPARENT TRACING PAPER,
EACH PATTERN COMES WITH A 8" x 10" BLACK AND WHITE PRINT OF THE FINISHED PROJECT.
THE LARGER SIZE PATTERNS ABOVE SELL FOR $6.95 EACH OR 3 FOR $18.95**

ALSO AVAILABLE;

TWO POSTER PATTERN SETS, "THE HIDDEN FOREST" AND "NEW SHOES" EACH SET COMES WITH A PATTERN
AND A 19" x 25 " FULL COLOR POSTER SUITABLE FOR FRAMING. $24.95 EACH.

A 90 MINUTE INTARSIA INSTRUCTIONAL VIDEO WHICH COVERS A BEGINNER LEVEL PATTERN FROM START TO
FINISH. $32.95

SCROLL SAW • FRETWORK PATTERN BOOKS
THE "FINE LINE DESIGN" BOOK SERIES

DESIGN BOOK #1	DESIGN BOOK #2	DESIGN BOOK #3
A GENERAL SUBJECT BOOK OF PATTERNS, FROM COWS TO PELICANS. $14.95	"WESTERN AND SOUTHWESTERN" PATTERNS OF COWBOYS, INDIANS, AND EVERYTHING IN BETWEEN. $16.95	"THE GREAT OUTDOORS" PATTERNS OF OUTDOOR SCENES FROM FISHING TO HOT AIR BALLOONS. $14.95

Take a Look at Our Other Fine Woodworking Books